DAY WALKER

28 HIKES

in the New York Metropolitan Area

DAY WALKER

28 HIKES
in the New York Metropolitan Area

by The New York/New Jersey Trail Conference

Edited by WALTER HOUCK

Text Coordinator   Arlene Coccari
Maps Coordinator   Roger Coco
Artist   Richard Edes Harrison

ANCHOR BOOKS
Anchor Press/Doubleday
Garden City, New York
1983

This paperback edition is the first publication of
DAY WALKER: 28 Hikes in the New York Metropolitan Area.
Anchor Books edition: 1983

Library of Congress Cataloging in Publication Data
Main entry under title:

Day walker.

1. Hiking—New York Metropolitan Area—Guide-books.
2. New York Metropolitan Area—Description—
Guide-books. I. Houck, Walter. II. New York/New
Jersey Trail Conference.
       GV199.42.N652N483   1983   917.47

ISBN: 0-385-14140-8
Library of Congress Catalog Card Number 79-7688
Copyright © 1983 by the New York/New Jersey Trail Conference, Inc.
All Rights Reserved
Printed in the United States of America
First Edition

CONTENTS

WALKING IN THE GREATER
NEW YORK METROPOLITAN AREA:
An Introduction

A sun-tanned, middle-aged man sits on a rock. He is nibbling on raisins and nuts, and his pack lies on the rock beside him. The Hudson River is almost at his feet; waves wash the multicolored pebbles at the base of the rock. Overhead, behind him, loom the massive cliffs of the Palisades. On the other side of the river, so remote that they are almost dreamlike, are the apartment towers and the factories of lower Westchester County. The air throbs faintly with the hum of distant civilization, but few sounds reach him. The bark of a faraway dog suddenly opens in the air and just as suddenly vanishes. On the far shore, a train passes—a barely audible streak against the patchwork colors of trees in autumn. The waves, the call of the birds, the slightly salty breeze off the rushes, the warm sun on the rocks, and the faint urban hum . . . no people, no radios, no traffic. Would you believe you can walk here from the IND?

Now the scene shifts. A woman, not yet middle-aged and not so sun-tanned, stands on a sandy rise. A road runs down from the rise and through an overgrown field. Running up the road are two children, with a man walking behind.

"Mommy, Mommy!" shouts the girl. "We saw one, one of the birds with the black thing on his head, what do you call it—"

"It was a quail," says the boy, slightly older.

"It was a partridge," says the girl. Turning back to the man on the road, she calls scornfully, "Oh, Daddy, wasn't it a partridge? Say it was a partridge. Please."

The father shakes his head and starts to explain that "quail" and "partridge" are two different names for the same group of birds, and that what they saw was probably a bobwhite, the local variety. But childish brows are furrowing, and the father decides to shift gears.

"Hey, who wants to see the ruined mansion? It's right down this other road." The kids yelp and are off running. This family is twelve minutes away from Queens, in Long Island's Muttontown Preserve.

The metropolitan area—including the five boroughs of New York City and the counties of Nassau, Suffolk, Westchester, Rockland, Passaic, Bergen, Union, Morris, Essex, and Middlesex—is full of such areas. This book presents a sample. All are open to the public. All are within 60 road miles of the George Washington Bridge, and many are much closer. Most can be reached by public transportation.

In difficulty these walks vary from easy to moderate; in length from a quarter of a mile to five miles, with a few being longer. Some of the walks have been popular for years; others have been so recently established that they are almost unknown.

The areas through which the walks pass are as varied as the walks themselves. Here are mountains, glacial moraines, salt marshes, ponds, lakes, rivers, and meadows. Here, too, are such man-made surroundings as an aqueduct, estates, a canal, abandoned rail roadbeds, and ancient woods roads and country lanes.

The walk descriptions contain information on geology, history, flora and fauna, bird watching, and Indian lore, as well as on the pleasures and techniques of walking itself. Although the book is written for the walker, many of these excursions will also interest the jogger, cross-country skier, bicyclist, bird watcher, and photographer.

This book has been written with detailed instructions on how to find a trail and how to follow it. For some, even more information will be needed. These people will probably want to walk with one of the many hiking clubs in the area; information is given on some of the clubs and how to find them.

The walker should be aware that the detailed instructions may become outdated. Roads change, and so do trails. During the period of the preparation of this book, almost every walk had to be altered to incorporate changes that had taken place. To keep up with trail changes, experienced walkers read the *Trail Walker*, the hikers' newspaper for the New York metropolitan area. *Trail Walker* is published by the New York/New Jersey Trail Conference (G.P.O. Box 2250, New York, NY 10001), which also produced this book.

If you find changes as you walk that have not yet been reported in the *Trail Walker*, take the initiative. Write the editor yourself. In this way others will be informed, and the information will also go into future editions of the book.

Walking is one of the simplest pastimes known. Any number and any age can participate, at any season. The necessary equipment is inexpensive and easily acquired. Many of the walks here are so short and simple that even the complete novice could take them with no preparation. Others are longer and more strenuous and require some knowledge of the outdoors. Some of the techniques are demonstrated in the first walk of this book, on the Palisades Shore Path.

Palisades

The long and spectacular cliffs of the Palisades line the west shore of the Hudson River all the way from the Tappan Zee to New York Harbor. Footpaths follow both the top and the bottom of the cliffs from the George Washington Bridge to the New York state line. This six-mile walk passes through the most scenic and least developed section of this stretch, following the Shore Path from the Alpine Boat Basin up to the state line.

This is not an easy walk for the complete novice. Some preparation is required. Here is how one walker might prepare for this kind of walk.

About three days before the trip I begin listening to weather forecasts on one of the all-news radio stations. When I learn that rain is expected on Friday but that Saturday will be clear, I decide to go to the Palisades. This is an early spring walk; if the weather has been too dry, the risk of fire might mean that the woods will be closed. The rain on Friday means that the woods will be dampened and safe.

During lunch hour on Friday, umbrella in hand, I visit the neighborhood outdoor store and the corner delicatessen to stock up on lunch items. At the copy center I make two photocopies of my walk map: one for me and one for a neighbor who will call park officials if I don't return on time.

Packing begins the night before the walk, with a trip to the refrigerator. There, grouped in a corner for convenience, are the perishable essentials: flashlight, camera film, raisin-nut-chocolate mixture in a plastic bottle, and tea bags. I add my day's purchases to the group, so that next morning everything will be together.

The next step is to use the bus schedule and map to calculate a

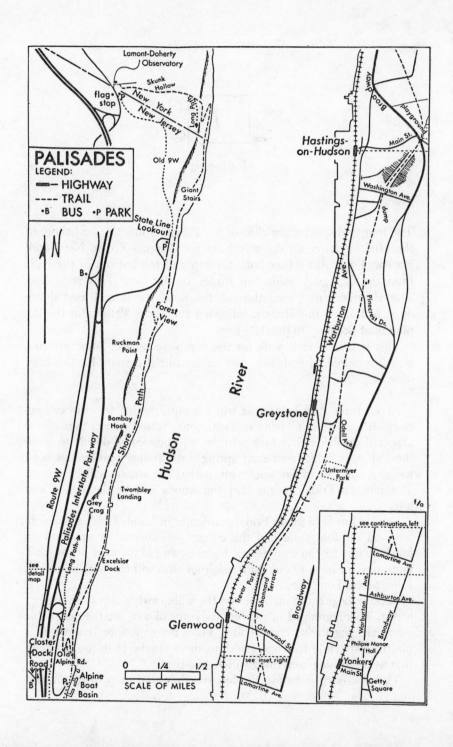

PALISADES
LEGEND:
▬▬ HIGHWAY
--- TRAIL
•B BUS •P PARK

Lamont-Doherty Observatory
Skunk Hollow
flag stop •P
New York
New Jersey
Long Path
Old 9W
Giant Stairs
State Line Lookout
•P
B•
Forest View
Ruckman Point
Shore Path
Bombay Hook
Palisades Interstate Parkway
Route 9W
Twombley Landing
Grey Crag
Long Path
Excelsior Dock
see detail map
Closter Dock Road
Old Alpine Rd.
•B
•P
Alpine Boat Basin

Hudson River

N

Hastings-on-Hudson
Saw Mill Brook
playground
Main St.
Washington Ave.
dump
Pinecrest Dr.
Warburton Ave.
Greystone
Odell Ave.
Untermyer Park
f/o

Trevor Park
Shonnard Terrace
Glenwood St.
Broadway
Glenwood
see inset, right
Lamartine Ave.

see continuation, left
Lamartine Ave.
Ashburton Ave.
Warburton Ave.
Broadway
Philipse Manor Hall
Yonkers
Main St.
Getty Square

0   1/4   1/2
SCALE OF MILES

pace and distance that will end the walk in time to catch the bus back to the city. Some parts of the Shore Path make for slow walking, so I figure to cover about two miles an hour. An easier walk—the Croton Aqueduct, for example—can be covered comfortably at three miles an hour. This is about a six-mile walk, a good distance for an early spring toner. Later in the season I might try the entire distance from the bridge; but if I were out of shape I might try only about three miles and stay on the path on top of the cliffs to cut out the strenuous climb.

The last task before going to bed is to tape a note and the map to my friendly neighbor's door, giving expected return time and the park phone number. When you walk alone, make sure to check in and out with a dependable person.

The morning of the walk, I warm up some leftovers for lunch and pour them into the vacuum bottle. While listening to the radio for the latest weather report, I fill the canteen with tap water. Spring water in the metropolitan area may be lovely to look at, but it can't be trusted for drinking.

Then I go to the two day packs that sit on the floor of the hall closet. The canteen and the vacuum bottle go into the first pack, along with the flashlight and snacks from the refrigerator. The front pocket of the first is packed with the items that ride on every trip:

- cup and spoon
- matches and candle
- insect repellent
- first aid and snakebite kits
- anti-blister patches
- scissors
- a traveler's check
- elastic bandage
- compass
- pocket knife and nail file
- 20 feet of heavy nylon (para-chute) cord
- kerchief
- toilet paper

In the back pouch of the pack with the vacuum bottle, canteen, and flashlight are a folding stove, camera, and towel. Much of this gear has never been used on any trip, but in an isolated area like the farther reaches of the Palisades a walker has to be prepared. I also throw in a paperback book to read on the ride to the walk.

The second pack on the floor is useful when walking with a companion, but its basic purpose is storage. The gear here is moved to the first pack and carried when conditions require it: extra canteens, light folding sun hat, mittens, a pullover cap, sunglasses, a sweater, a rain poncho, and a windbreaker.

Dress consists of jeans, a T-shirt, a wool shirt, and a vest (recycled from an otherwise worn-out business suit). Another recycled item is my pair of shoes. Hiking boots are used by many walkers, particularly in a rocky place like the Palisades, but sturdy rubber-soled shoes that have become too worn for office use, such as oxfords, are preferred by many people for their comfort and light weight.

THE WALK

This is a through walk. We will be returning to the city by bus from a point many miles from the beginning. Car drivers on through walks have to find a way back to their cars. They have three choices.

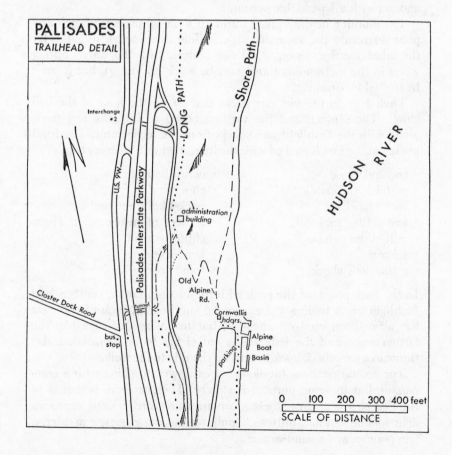

The first is to return to the beginning of the walk by bus. The second is to convert the walk to a loop, say, by going as far as Forest View and then returning to Alpine by the Shore Path or the Long Path. The third is to use two cars, if available. Meet at the parking lot on the old route of Highway 9W at the entrance to Lamont-Doherty Observatory. Leaving one car there, all the walkers go back to Alpine in the other car. Walk through to the car at the observatory and drive back to Alpine.

By bus, the trip to Alpine from the George Washington Bridge Terminal on the Red & Tan bus takes less than half an hour. Service is frequent and the cost is low. The bus is often crowded, so plan on being a little early if you want a seat.

Leave the bus at Closter Dock Road. About fifty yards north of the stop, a tunnel on the east side of Highway 9W takes pedestrians under the Palisades Interstate Parkway. On the far side, pick up the path curving left and running parallel to the parkway. Note the blue blazes; this is the Long Path, which goes all the way from the George Washington Bridge to the Catskills.

Follow the Long Path through an underpass under a paved road, which is the park drive down to the Alpine Boat Basin. Just past the underpass, turn right on an old woods road. A few hundred feet later, another woods road heads down to the left. Turn downhill on this, which is the Old Alpine Road. In 1776 the Old Alpine Road was used by British troops on their march to cut off an isolated American garrison in Fort Lee after the main American force under Washington had made its retreat to distant White Plains.

Via a series of sweeping curves the cobblestone road descends toward the Hudson. At times the docks and picnic area below can be seen through the foliage. Near the bottom, the Old Alpine Road ends at another road, bordered by a chain link fence. Here a sign indicates the direction of the Shore Trail, another name for the Shore Path. This walk will go to the left, but I take a short detour down to the picnic tables of the marina to the right. Walkers arriving by car will be starting the walk at the parking lot here, which is off Interchange 2 of the Palisades Interstate Parkway, 7 miles north of the George Washington Bridge.

For those of us with sensitive feet, here is a good place to attend to them. If I feel any burning on my soles or toes during the descent, off comes the shoe and on goes the adhesive Moleskin anti-blister

pad. While I cut a piece out of the pad, my small folding Sterno stove will boil a cup of tea.

A simple white house sits at the edge of the picnic area under the cliff. Houses like this once lined the river shore, back when roads were poor and the river was the main transport route. Now only this house remains, preserved because for a few hours the British general Cornwallis relaxed here while his troops toiled to pull wagons and cannons up the road we just came down.

Finishing tea, I pull off the vest, folding it and putting it in my knapsack. Walking creates a lot of body heat, even on a cool day. By wearing many layers of clothes, walkers can add on or peel down to maintain comfort. Then I set out.

The trail angles up the slope along the fence, passing the end of the Old Alpine Road. Along the side of the trail are small patches of turquoise paint that mark the route. Most of the trails in the metropolitan area are marked in some way: by paint blazes, by wooden posts, by concrete markers, even by colored metal disks, depending on who did the marking. Trails blazed by the New York/New Jersey Trail Conference follow a standard scheme. Each path in an area has its own color, to distinguish it from other trails in the vicinity. Two blazes together indicate a turn, with the top blaze offset in the direction of a turn. Three blazes in a triangle pattern indicate the end of a trail.

The trail soon crosses a gorge on a massive stone bridge. Beneath, a tiny stream trickles over moss-covered rocks. The trail is already some fifty feet up the slope from the Hudson. Soon after, the trail leaves a set of steps and comes to a fork. A picnic area is ahead on the left; on the right the Shore Path descends to the shore at Excelsior Dock.

Now that the trail has returned to the shore, it will stay by the water for more than a mile. The path is level and wide, and the footing is mostly hard dirt. This section was rebuilt in 1980–81. Now it is a little too roadlike for some walkers, but a few years should return it to a more natural condition. Towering above is the isolated cliff column known as Grey Crag. The shore curves in and out, with reeds on the points of land.

Twombley Landing is a square landfill pier jutting out into the Hudson. It is named for the family that once lived here. Grey Crag now looms directly overhead. Just around the point, the Tappan Zee

Bridge comes into view. A mile ahead on the left is another crag,
Bombay Hook. Its name comes from the Dutch word *boomje*,
"small tree." This stretch of cliffs between Grey Crag and Bombay
Hook is the longest uninterrupted stretch in the Palisades. Many
people, hearing of trails in the Palisades, imagine an airy cliffside ad-
venture. In fact, much of the Palisades is wooded from top to bottom. The trails up and down the cliffs use these wooded slopes.
There are no trails in the open cliffs at all, because the rock is too
fragile to support them.

Everywhere along the trail are signs of humanity: fireplaces, foundations, abandoned piers. But humanity itself is distant. Across the
river, tiny trains shuttle from station to station. Ships and barges
pass on the river. Occasional sounds break through the general hum
of civilization: dogs barking, factory whistles, motorcycles, airplanes.

From Grey Crag at one end to Bombay Hook at the other takes
about a half hour of walking. Beyond, further sections of cliff rise
above the trail in isolated splendor: Ruckman Point, at 520 feet
above the water, is the highest. Finally the path comes around a
bush-covered point with a large weeping willow over the water. High
bramble bushes crowd the trail. This is Forest View, once a popular
picnic area. Now, picnic tables float in a sea of brambles. A tall wire
structure sticks out of the foliage; one is startled to realize it is a
baseball backstop.

At Forest View the wide path ends. A marked trail turning uphill
leads to the Long Path and to the parking lot and refreshment stand
at State Line Lookout. To avoid the rough walking ahead, some
walkers may prefer to take this cutoff, continuing to the state-line bus
stop by following the Long Path or the old route of Highway 9W.
Soon after, the square white blazes of the Shore Path angle off to
the left. Stay toward the water, watching for the white half-moon
blaze that marks the last part of the trail up to the state line. The
blazing is erratic, but, with the trail restricted to a narrow strip be-
ween cliff and river, getting lost is not a problem if the walker is
patient.

The pleasant walk through Forest View ends abruptly at a pile of
giant boulders that comes down to the water. Without crossing the
rockslide, the trail makes a sharp turn left and uphill. Here are round
white markers; the stones have been moved into a stairway to make
climbing easier. The trail keeps making jogs to the left, away from

the direction it should be going. Finally the path leads over a stone retaining wall and heads to the right. At this point the trail is above the boulder field, perhaps sixty feet up from the water.

For the next half mile the trail goes from rock to rock. If the blazes are difficult to follow, watch for broken branches, mud splashed up on rocks, and beaten-down dirt to indicate the route. In the half hour that this rock hopping requires, I think about safety. This stretch is supposedly home to poisonous copperhead snakes. Copperheads are notoriously slow and mild-mannered, but this knowledge does not appease me. Fortunately, in ten years of walking, I have yet to see a poisonous snake in the wild.

Many non-walkers are concerned about poisonous snakes and dangerous wild animals. This fear is usually misplaced. Snakebites cause fewer deaths in the United States than do bee stings. The only dangerous animal in most areas is *Homo sapiens*, a danger that can be avoided through prudence: staying out of parks after nightfall, not walking alone in remote areas if you are a woman.

The main safety concerns for the walker are not wildlife but weather and falls. Both cold and hot weather can be dangerous. Cold by itself is simple to prepare for, but cold combined with rain is not. A combination of temperature in the forty- to fifty-degree range, a light rain, and wind can be lethal. Rain also increases the chances of slipping. A thunderstorm can be lethal at any temperature. To cope with these dangers, avoid them; do not walk when the forecast indicates potential danger. For simple cold, wear extra clothes and carry a backpacker-type stove and warm fluids. Cut a walk short if necessary.

Hot weather is also a problem, particularly to those who are out to prove something by pushing themselves. I walk even on the hottest days, but I carry extra canteens, move slowly and keep to shade, wear a broad-brimmed light hat, and dress in shorts.

Safety as much as conviviality is the reason why many people prefer to walk with family, friends, or a hiking club. The metropolitan area has more than fifty hiking clubs, and most are usually looking for new members. Some of the clubs are small and informal; others are more elaborate than some small businesses, with publications, cabins, and a wide range of activities. To find a club to hike with, ask a hiking friend or write to the New York/New Jersey Trail Con-

2

ference, G.P.O. Box 2250, New York, NY 10001, and ask for the club list.

The path finally leaves the boulder-filled woods and leads out onto open rocks. The jumble of boulders is faded to a reddish tan by exposure; the red comes from the iron contained in the Palisades rock. The path descends an easily followed rock stairway, through a grove of trees, and then out onto another set of rock stairs that crosses an enormous rock slide. This descent is called the Giant Stairs. Here, I check my watch and itinerary and settle down to lunch.

After lunch I walk a few paces, turn around, and check the area. Satisfied that nothing is forgotten and no litter remains, I head north, through the woods on the other side of the rockslide. The trail descends another thirty feet to the edge of the Hudson. Here water can be heard dripping under the huge boulders that come down to the water's edge.

The smell of salt water is strong here. The trail passes a marshy area; bushes along the trail have dry pods that rattle when touched. The Tappan Zee is now close; the trail has crossed the state line into New York.

Soon after, the trail angles uphill from the river. No cliffs are visible from this point, just a heavily wooded steep slope. The path makes a switchback uphill and then another. Ladders help at the steepest spots. Finally, as the trail nears the top, the cliffs can be seen through the forest. Here they are green and moss-covered, all but buried in the foliage and only about thirty feet high; but they still have the distinctive column and spire structure.

The trail skirts the base of the cliffs and ducks into a hollow, Skunk Hollow, where the cliffs curve away. Here two other trails join. The trail to the right, with sloppy yellow dot markers, reaches a spectacular last viewpoint over the river in a few paces and then continues into the twenty-acre Lamont Nature Sanctuary. The sanctuary adjoins Lamont-Doherty Observatory, an important center for oceanographic research. The blue-blazed Long Path comes down a long rock stairway from the left and continues straight ahead.

A glance at my watch confirms that the bus is due soon—no time for any side trips into the sanctuary. The Long Path leads ahead directly to the bus stop. Continue northwest with the blue blazes, crossing a stream. On the other side of the stream, another Lamont trail joins from the right. The combined trail goes left (west) about an eighth of a mile along the stream. Then the yellow blazes curve away to the left, and the Long Path turns right and over a low hill. Ahead, a road can be seen: the old route of Highway 9W. Beyond is the sound of traffic. The Long Path comes out on a driveway, with Route 9W and the Lamont-Doherty Observatory gatehouse now in sight to the left; note the big "Welcome to New York" sign on the highway. Down to the left is the parking area on old 9W. Across the road the shoulder is paved; the bus back to New York will stop here when I flag it down.

—S. Fox

LONG ISLAND: For the Family

When the bud bursts green on the twig and the drone of the power mower fills the air, families start to think about a walk in the outdoors. Preparing for family walks is a skill, and Long Island is a good place to begin for the family with young and inexperienced walkers. The areas are small and the woods tend to be level, reducing the possibility of getting lost. Trails are sandy, with few rocks to catch young toes or cut stumbling bodies. The only problem of note is the possibility of acquiring a tick, so children should be warned to stay out of the brush and they should be inspected after a walk.

Equipment and preparation can be held to a minimum: a few snacks and a canteen. A more elaborate kit might include a bird or plant book and binoculars.

The simplicity of walking on Long Island does not mean that parents have to avoid the more rugged areas. It does mean that preparation and experience are required. Even very young children can be taken into any area within range of the day walker, if the adults have first scouted the trail and they respect the capabilities of their children.

Infants and toddlers can go almost anywhere in a carrier. A walk to them is just another outing on foot, like a shopping trip. Remember that the walkers are generating heat by their exercise but an infant is not and therefore may require warmer clothes. Otherwise the preparations are the same as those for any outing: a diaper, a towel, and perhaps some formula in the pouch under the seat of the child carrier. On longer outings a belt-style fanny pack is useful for carrying and getting at the necessary paraphernalia. Parents using strollers rather than carriers can also use trails, provided they head for the smooth paths of Caumsett State Park, or those of Manhattan's Riverside Park or the river section of the Hook Mountain walk in Rockland County.

The two-to-four group is more difficult to handle on an outing than the infants. Kids in this age group still have to be carried at least part of the way, but they're heavier. Their preferences are more

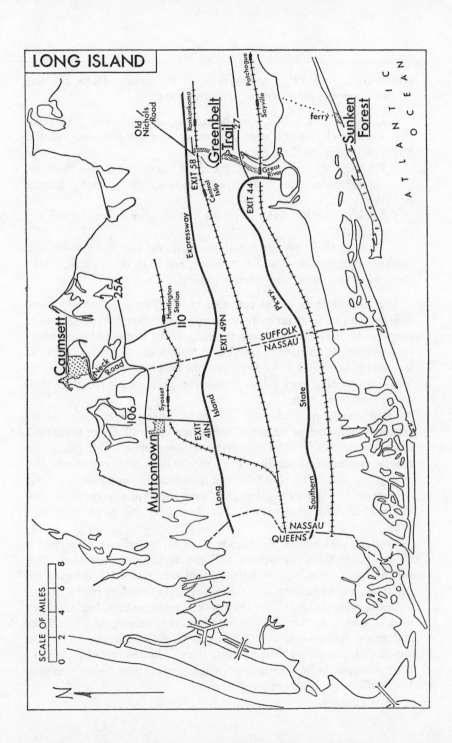

pronounced, and often more difficult to satisfy. Here are one mother's suggestions for coping with this age group:

1. CANDY (M & M's, sour balls, lollipops, anything with sugar that won't melt), to be used as a reward for distance covered, the completion of quiet time, etc.

2. Resting only on rocks with the child's name on them—these are rocks of particular sizes and shapes, and definitely at least a quarter or half mile apart.

3. Looking for the baby elephant (who's always just behind my two-year-old!).

4. Talking them up—asking them to be on the lookout for trail markers, telling them about the flowers and trees by the trail, asking them what they want for birthdays or Christmas.

The four-to-seven group can also be challenging. Some of these children can walk as far as their parents. But, like the younger ones, they can be fickle and unpredictable. Coaxing, stops, and games may be required. Be prepared to declare a walk finished when it looks as if the kids have had it for the day—but be prepared for the miraculous recovery that may follow a stop for candy or for dangling tired feet in a stream.

From seven on up through the teens, young people become increasingly stronger as walkers. Often they can walk faster than their parents, particularly after the first half hour or so. This group can handle greater responsibility. They should have their own packs and gear. They should be able to invite friends along, and they can have a voice in the pre-walk planning. Once they know enough to stop and wait at trail intersections, they should be able to set their own pace.

Walking with several children has its own techniques. One child is always faster than the others, and the slower ones get mad. This problem may be solved by letting them take turns. If your children squabble, letting each invite a friend may help to reduce conflicts.

Walks with children have their special requirements, but also their own benefits. For the children, walking gives training in self-reliance and group responsibility. Families can be active together, at a cost any family can afford. For parents, there's the opportunity to know their children better, from that magic time when young eyes and tiny hands begin to discover our world.

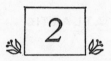

Fire Island—Sunken Forest

The Sunken Forest is a unique and fascinating natural area. Located within the Fire Island National Seashore, it is a cool, moist, and fragrant environment—an enchanting contrast to the sun, sand, and salt water of the nearby beach. From the ferry landing at Sailors Haven, you pass on boardwalks through stands of oak, pine, holly, and sassafras. The dunes are covered with bearberry, and small areas of marshland are tucked in among the thickets. Along the way, there are breathtaking views of ocean and bay. The entire walk takes less than an hour; afterward, there's sunning and swimming on Fire Island's uncrowded beaches.

It is easy to reach this area by public transport. From New York City and western Long Island, go by Long Island Rail Road to Sayville, then by taxi to the ferry terminal on River Road. Here the ferry takes you to Sailors Haven. The distance from the George Washington Bridge to Sayville is 55 miles, and the trip from Penn Station takes approximately an hour and a half. For taxi service in Sayville, call Colonial Taxi at (516) 588-7878 or 589-7878.

If you have time and are feeling ambitious, you can walk the mile from the station through the old village of Sayville to the ferry. Walk south from the station on Lakeland Avenue (also called Railroad Avenue). Cross Main Street (Montauk Highway) and continue south on the same street you were on, which is now called Gillette Avenue. When this street ends, turn left on Edwards Street to Foster Avenue, where you turn right. At the intersection of Foster Avenue with Terry Street is a Fire Island Ferry sign. Follow the sign directing you left on Terry Street to River Road. Turn right here. The ferry terminal and parking lot are on the left.

If coming by car, take Exit 59 south on the Long Island Expressway. Go south on Ocean Avenue and bear left on Lakeland Avenue

(Route 93), crossing Veterans Highway, Sunrise Highway, and the Long Island Rail Road tracks. From there, the directions are the same as those above for walkers. A small fee is charged for parking in the ferry terminal's parking lot.

The ferry from Sayville to Sailors Haven on Fire Island runs from May through October. The schedule for spring and fall is different from the summer schedule. (Winter access, unfortunately, is possible only for those prepared to walk east about ten miles or so from Robert Moses State Park, which has the nearest bridge from Long Island.) For current ferry schedule information, telephone (516) 589-1844 during the day and (516) 472-1313 evenings. To obtain a schedule, write the National Seashore Ferry, Inc., 10 Brown's River

Road, Bayport, Long Island, NY 11705. When you purchase your ticket, make sure you have a schedule so that you can plan your return trip.

(It is possible that within the next few years the National Park Service will establish its own ferry service to Sailors Haven. Patchogue may be the other terminus of this service. Patchogue is accessible from the same branch of the Long Island Rail Road that serves Sayville. Call the National Park Service at [516] 289-4810 for current information.)

I enjoy taking the earliest ferry. The forest seems especially fresh, clean, and quiet in the early morning. The ferry trip to Sailors Haven is a pleasant ride of twenty minutes across the Great South Bay. Sit on the upper deck to observe the "clammers" working from their squat little boats. On a clear day the Captree Bridge is visible to the west. This bridge provides access from Long Island to Captree State Park and Boat Basin, Jones Beach, and Robert Moses State Park.

As you approach Sailors Haven, Fire Island stretches east and west before you. Well over a dozen communities dot its thirty-two-mile length. Most of them can be reached by ferry from Bay Shore, Sayville, or Patchogue. The National Seashore has acquired nearly twenty miles of ocean front. Three facilities have been developed: Smith Point West, Watch Hill, and Sailors Haven. In addition there are county parks, including Smith Point County Park at the eastern end of the island, and a state park, Robert Moses State Park, at the western end of the island.

Fire Island (also called Great South Beach) is a barrier beach formed after the retreat of the last ice sheet ten thousand years ago. Currents and waves formed sand bars, which eventually joined to form a continuous stretch of sand. Today, this is a constantly shifting environment, where land accumulation and erosion occur simultaneously. Storms tear at the island. Dunes are eroded, and sand is blown and washed away. Every year houses are lost to the sea. In the winter the beach is narrow, as the sand washes offshore to form a bar. In the summer the beaches widen again as the sand returns.

The ferry ride terminates at Sailors Haven, where there is a boat marina, with docks and boardwalks. The building to your left is a snack bar and small store where food, souvenirs, boating essentials, tanning lotions, and Fire Island guides and newspapers are sold.

Directly ahead and up the stairs is the visitors' center, including a small museum. Stop here to obtain a free copy of the Fire Island National Seashore brochure. You can also purchase a booklet called *Exploring Sunken Forest*. The booklet describes the forest walk. Markers along the trail correspond to numbered descriptions in the booklet.

As you leave the visitors' center, turn left (facing the bay) to reach the forest boardwalk. Follow it a few paces along the bay, past a large boardwalk to the beach and a second boardwalk leading to an area where outdoor programs are held. The forest boardwalk soon veers to the left and enters the woods. To protect yourself and the environment, stay on the boardwalk. Poison ivy, with its three shiny leaves (red in autumn, green in spring and summer), grows everywhere. The thorny vine with heart-shaped leaves is cat brier.

The forest in many places seems impenetrable. Occasional eroded spots are passed. Much of this erosion was caused by foot traffic before the boardwalk was built.

Although you may not see them, many animals live in the forest. Early one morning I saw a doe and a fawn resting quietly in the dunes. Foxes have also been seen. The air is alive with the constant motion and call of birds, including catbirds, warblers, towhees, and brown thrashers.

Near the boardwalk grow sassafras trees, with their deeply ridged reddish-brown bark and leaves with one, two, or three lobes. Holly trees of great age and size also grow here. Notice how the trunks and limbs of many of the trees are twisted and contorted, mute testimony to the harshness of the natural environment.

You will leave the forest temporarily. Here, at the first lookout and the first steps, you can see along the ocean the line of dunes that protect the forest from the harsh salty wind and make its growth possible. Notice the low, thick patches of bearberry growing on the dunes. Bearberry, an evergreen, has white flowers in the spring and red berries in the fall.

Soon the trail turns right and up another series of steps to a lookout. Here the platform gives a view over both the ocean and the bay. Most of the foliage seems to be neatly clipped; very little grows higher than the thirty-foot-high protective dunes along the ocean. The salt in the air kills nearly everything that attempts to grow

Fire Island National Seashore, dune walk

higher. The one exception is the red cedar, which is highly resistant
to the salt concentration.

Standing here, with the sea breeze and the intricate and delicate
forest flowing away to the dunes, and the vast ocean beyond, is
sufficient in itself to make this trip worthwhile.

From the overlook in the treetops, return to the forest, where you
will see a large stand of old holly trees. The oldest holly here is approximately a hundred and seventy-five years old.

The boardwalk passes through a salt marsh, where the tall *Phragmites* reed grows. Go straight ahead to the platform on the Great
South Bay. If it isn't foggy, you can see Long Island from here. Backtrack from this point and turn right almost immediately. The boardwalk now passes over a fresh-water bog, where cattails rustle dryly in
the breeze. Then it re-enters the forest, soon passing benches on the
right. You may want to stay a few minutes here to rest and view before continuing.

Your departure from the forest is marked by a large stone on your
left, with a memorial plaque:

A PRIMEVAL HOLLY FOREST

A sanctuary for wildlife: a field for study by scientists and lovers
of nature, a retreat for the refreshment of the human spirit. Enter
here to enjoy, but not to injure or destroy.

Follow the boardwalk away from the woods. Take the cement
walk (note the comfort station at the ninety-degree bend here) until
you reach a boardwalk that stretches from forest to ocean. From here
there are two ways back to Sailors Haven and the ferry back to
Sayville.

The first is to continue along the sidewalk between the forest and
the dunes. This will bring you back to the main boardwalk between
marina and beach, in the area where the cold showers and rest rooms
are located and where swimmers can change into their bathing suits.
This path offers an interesting perspective on the forest from the
outside.

The second is to turn right, crossing the dunes on the boardwalk.
Follow the steps down to the beach. Here you can stop to relax,
beachcomb, and wade. If you wade, stay between the flags, where the
lifeguards are stationed.

A short walk along the beach west will bring you to Point O' Woods. This is an old and dignified community of brown-shingled homes, where signs of wealth are evident.

The first community in the other direction, past the swimming area, is Cherry Grove. Cherry Grove is a village with its own unique liberated flavor, quite in contrast to Point O' Woods.

For your walk through the forest, insect repellent is essential at certain times of the year, when mosquitoes are extremely bothersome. The park service suggests that sneakers or other footwear be worn on the boardwalks, so that slivers can be avoided.

Bring field glasses if you have them. It will add a new dimension to your experience. If you haven't had extensive exposure to the sun, a sun-screen lotion and hat are essential. Bring a bathing suit and beach towel.

A small day pack or tote bag to carry the above items, plus lunch and drink, will make your trip easier. I prefer a day pack, so that my hands will be free to pick up stones and shells on the beach and so that my field glasses are handy for birding and horizon watching. Some way of carrying gear also makes life easier if you decide to extend your walk with an exploration of Sayville.

Sayville is one village in this part of Long Island whose downtown shopping area has not been destroyed by nearby shopping centers. There are several places to eat, antique and craft shops, clothing stores, florists, and a superb bookstore. Most of the shops are on or near Main Street (Montauk Highway).

The Sayville area was once occupied by Secatogue Indians. In 1697 the land was given to William Nicholls by King William III of England.

The first tenant of what is now Sayville village was John Edwards, who built a house here in 1761.

The oldest house still standing was built in 1785; it is now the home of the Sayville Historical Society. It is located at the corner of Edwards and Collins streets. You will pass it on your way to or from the ferry. The museum is open during the summer on Wednesday and Saturday afternoons.

The Sunken Forest offers an easy walk which should be taken quietly and unhurriedly, so that the sights, sounds, and smells of the forest and ocean can be enjoyed. My favorite times here are spring and late summer through early fall. These are quieter, less frantic times, with fewer boats and people. You may find, as I have, that you will return to this sanctuary often, to refresh the spirit and to enjoy the beach and forest in all its seasons, moods, and colors.

—ARLENE COCCARI

Long Island Greenbelt Trail

To discover Long Island as it was centuries ago, walk the Long Island Greenbelt Trail. A particularly interesting six-mile day walk on the trail runs from Union Boulevard in Great River north to Johnson Avenue in Ronkonkoma. This one-way route follows the Connetquot River through the 3,500-acre Connetquot River State Park to the headwaters of the river in Lakeland County Park.

The walk takes about four hours at a leisurely pace. Elevation ranges from sea level to twenty-five feet, and the ground is soft and sandy. Sneakers are fine except in wet weather. Much of the terrain is covered with huckleberry and other shrubs, so long pants are advisable to avoid scratches on narrow side paths.

The trail operates on a reservation/permit system, which means you call ahead to the park at (516) 581-1005 before starting. At the entrance booth of the Connetquot River State Park on Sunrise Highway, about a mile east of the intersection of Connetquot Road and Sunrise Highway, you'll be given a free map and permit to cross the park. Plan to arrive after 8 A.M. and before 3 P.M. to receive the permit, and do not come on Monday, since at this writing the park is closed then.

The trail is easily reached from anywhere on Long Island and the metropolitan area. It is 50 miles east of the George Washington Bridge, a drive of about an hour and a half via the Southern State Parkway or Long Island Expressway. On hot summer weekends, finish your walk at an early hour to avoid the beach traffic.

For car users, either end of the walk is equally convenient, but there is no easy way except backtracking to return to the starting point. The southern end is reached from Exit 44 of the Southern State Parkway: take Route 27 (Sunrise Highway) east to Connetquot Avenue (Great River Road) and turn right (south) to the

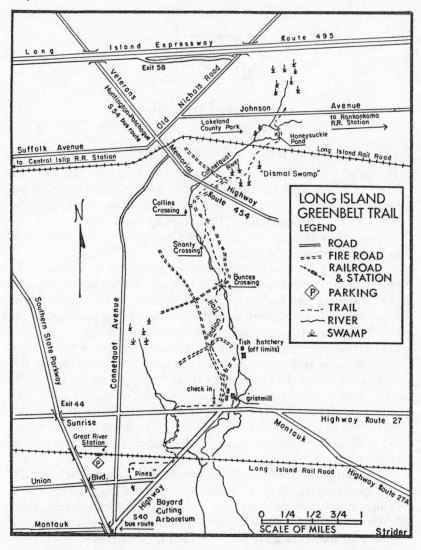

Great River railroad station. The northern end is near Exit 58 of the Long Island Expressway: go south from the exit on Old Nichols Road to Johnson Avenue. Turn left (east) on Johnson Avenue and go three quarters of a mile to Lakeland County Park. From either end, the walk out to Bunces Crossing and back makes for about a six-mile trip. If coming from the north, remember that you will first have to visit the Connetquot Park entrance booth on Sunrise Highway for a permit.

Walkers relying on public transportation have several options, involving various combinations of bus, train, and cab. Most walkers coming from points west will be taking the Long Island Rail Road to the Great River station on the Montauk line. For details of the other options and a free map of the entire Greenbelt Trail, send a stamped, self-addressed envelope to the Long Island Greenbelt Trail Conference at 23 Deer Path Road, Center Islip, Long Island, NY 11722.

Now let's start the walk. From the Great River station, walk one block south on Connetquot Avenue to Union Boulevard. A short distance east (left) on Union Boulevard, you will see the state road sign for a trail crossing: a green and white highway sign showing two hikers with staffs and backpacks.

The white-blazed trail heading north from this crossing immediately enters a woods. This forgotten stretch of parkland is a botanical feast. Mosses, grasses, and wild berries cover the forest floor. The trail winds around giant oaks and stands of larch and white pines. Just before the railroad crossing the trail leads through a plantation of young pines that is especially beautiful in the snow.

Leaving the pines at Montauk Highway, walk single file along the bridge over the railroad tracks. (Or, if you have an extra hour or two and the price of admission, you can carefully cross the highway to visit the meadows and gardens of the Bayard Cutting Arboretum.) At the far end of the bridge, follow the blazes across a large meadow.

At the end of the meadow is a levee bordering a stream, West Brook. Follow the trail across the stream over a small concrete dam. The dam was built in the late nineteenth century; the pond behind it was used extensively for ice production before the era of refrigeration. Now it hosts mallards, Canadian geese, swans, egrets, kingfishers, trout, eels, and snapping turtles. Mountain laurel, skunk cabbage, cat brier, and Canada mayflowers grow along its shores. Follow the white blazes along the shore of the pond and cross under Sunrise Highway, using the walkway under the bridge at the north end.

A short distance east on Sunrise Highway is the entrance to Connetquot River State Park. Get your permit and ask for a map at the

entrance booth. Just ahead on the right is a gristmill. Built by the
Nicholls family, it dates from the early 1700s. At that time, all the
land in this vicinity was part of William Nicholls' Islip Grange. This
51,000-acre tract was the largest manor on Long Island. Nicholls
purchased his first land from Chief Winnequaheagh of the Connetquot Indians in 1683.

The narrow road running past the buildings and the mill is the
original South Country Road. It was laid out in 1733 and for many
years was the only east-west road on the south shore. An important
stagecoach route, it was traveled by George Washington on his historic tour of Long Island in 1790.

The main building was originally an inn, built in 1820 by Elipha-
let Snedicor. The area was renowned for its hunting and fishing, and
in 1866 a group of wealthy men purchased the inn and surrounding
acreage and formed the South Side Sportsmen's Club. Many
members, including W. K. Vanderbilt, Commodore F. G. Bourne,
and W. Bayard Cutting, built opulent estates along the Great South
Bay. The club used, maintained, and protected the land for over a
hundred years. Then the state purchased it and in 1973 opened the
Connetquot River State Park.

Follow the trail north, taking care not to wander from the blazed
path. At first it passes through an open woods, then follows a paved
road that after a mile or so becomes a dirt way. Watch for deer,
which seem quite unafraid of quiet people. There are also chipmunks, wild turkeys, turtles, ospreys (several nesting pairs), great
blue herons, egrets, and a variety of hawks. Even bald eagles have
been spotted in the park, as have winter wrens, brown creepers, wood
ducks, and nesting bluebirds.

The terrain is flat and sandy, and most of the 3,500 acres is filled
with low-bush and high-bush huckleberry, blueberry, and tiny win-
tergreen under stands of pitch pine and oak. The pitch pine is especially suited to this terrain. The sandy soil drains water quickly, so
that the vegetation is usually dry. Forest fires are common; you
should spot at least one burned-over area before reaching Bunces
Crossing. Oaks are usually killed by fire, but most pitch pines survive
because of their thick bark. In addition, fire causes the cones of the
pitch pine to open and release their seeds.

The trail eventually leaves the road and enters the stretch named
by trailworkers the "Indian Trail." The foliage here becomes more

diverse because of the trail's proximity to the river. This area is especially beautiful in September and early October. Look for ferns, swamp maples, bayberry, inkberry, and blueberry.

Long Island Indians stayed along the rivers in the woods during the cold winter months and moved to the shore to fish and clam during the summer. The tribes of Long Island were renowned for their wampum, money carved from the abundant clam and whelk shells of the south shore. One translation of Paumanouk, an Indian name for Long Island, is "Isle of Tribute." Whenever fierce tribes from the mainland threatened war, the peace-loving Indians of Long Island were able to buy them off with payments of their beautiful wampum.

The trail crosses the Connetquot River at Bunces Crossing, named for the man who helped build the original bridge. This is the only spot in the park past the entrance where the main trail actually comes to the river, which makes this a good spot to enjoy lunch and a rest break at the grassy clearings along the river's edge. The crossing is the turnaround point for many out-and-back hikers. You can probably catch a glimpse of trout released into the river from the nearby fish hatchery. Trout thrive in the cool, clear, and very clean waters. The Connetquot River is almost entirely ground water and is well protected by the surrounding parkland.

Heading north from the crossing, watch for a series of clearings containing only large pines and no undergrowth. These areas date from 1890, when the South Side Sportsmen's Club began planting grain to attract quail. Remnants still remain of the fences that were used to keep out the deer.

A side trail soon comes up that leads back to the river at Shanty Crossing. A mile or so later, another side trail to the left leads over to Collins Crossing. In May, be sure to take the short detour to this crossing to see and smell the large patch of lilies of the valley. A park caretaker's house formerly stood on this location, where a carriage road once crossed the river.

Farther north, back on the main trail where it detours to the west of the main dirt road, look for the recently discovered remnants (a raised, moss-covered mound) of an old north-south carriage road that was once used by south-shore residents to reach the early Long Island Rail Road.

Shortly after the trail crosses Veterans Memorial Highway, you'll cross a narrow paved road. This is a remaining portion of Old Wheelers Road, an early farm-to-market route from Central Islip to Bayport. (This road is an alternate route to end the walk; a half mile to the left is the intersection of Veterans Memorial Highway and Old Nichols Road, where a public telephone to call a cab can be found at the gas station.) The white blazes continue across the road and soon come to a low wet area affectionately dubbed "Dismal Swamp" by the muddy and tired trail builders who put down the planks you are walking on. Ten minutes ahead are the tracks of the Long Island's Ronkonkoma line. This was the first line built and was completed to Greenport in 1844. (It's said that the service was faster and better then!) The Ronkonkoma station is a mile and a half east and the Central Islip station is a mile and a quarter west from this point.

Continue across the tracks into Lakeland County Park. This area was once slated to be an industrial development. In 1969 a bulldozer had actually begun to fill in Honeysuckle Pond, before local citizens stopped the work by sitting down in the bulldozer's path. The beach you are walking on is the scar from the excavation. Now the land all belongs to Suffolk County as Lakeland County Park, the last stop on this brief excursion into Long Island's past.

Several hundred yards past Honeysuckle Pond is a side road to a campsite area, with a parking lot. Rest rooms and a telephone may be available here, depending on the season. The road ahead leads out to the park's main entrance on Johnson Avenue and the end of the walk.

The Greenbelt land was purchased over time by the state, county, and local municipalities in order to protect the watershed of the two rivers from contamination from the surrounding densely populated suburbs. The tract varies in width from seventy-five feet to one mile. The trail dates from 1976, when a group of local citizens won the support of government officials for the creation of a hiking trail crossing the island along the Greenbelt. The Long Island Greenbelt Trail Conference was formed to map, blaze, and maintain the trail. The trail it opened is unique: it follows two separate entire river systems, with numerous historic sites, and features the habitats of almost every plant and animal to be found anywhere on Long Island.

—NANCY DIEHL MANFREDONIA

Caumsett State Park

Isolated on the Lloyd Neck peninsula, Caumsett State Park encompasses the 1,500-acre former estate of Marshall Field III. Here one can observe shore birds at the salt marsh, enjoy a grand view of Long Island Sound from the mansion, or ramble along miles of trails through pastoral scenery or along the beach. The walk described here is about seven miles long, but shorter walks are easily fashioned. Cross-country skiers use the park's trails during the winter months. The park also offers, by advance registration, a variety of special guided programs. There are plans to establish a riding stable. All trails are level and smooth; the main loop from the parking area to the mansion is paved.

The park is open from 8 A.M. to 4:30 P.M. every day of the year except Christmas and New Year's Day. A limited number of fishing permits are available by advance registration; applications may be secured at any state park. Dogs are not permitted.

If you are using public transportation, take the Long Island Rail Road from Penn Station. At the station, taxis are available for the long (eight miles) and expensive trip to the park. Don't forget to arrange for the return trip with the driver. A public telephone is available at the dairy complex adjacent to the parking area.

If you are coming by car, the park is 45 miles from the George Washington Bridge. Take the Long Island Expressway to Exit 49N. Continue north for several miles on Route 110 across Route 25 to Huntington. Turn left on Main Street (Route 25A), go three blocks, and turn right on West Neck Road. Follow West Neck Road onto Lloyd Harbor Road to the park entrance. A nominal fee is charged for parking. Street parking is not allowed on the roads outside the park.

A few words of caution: ticks are present here as they are else-

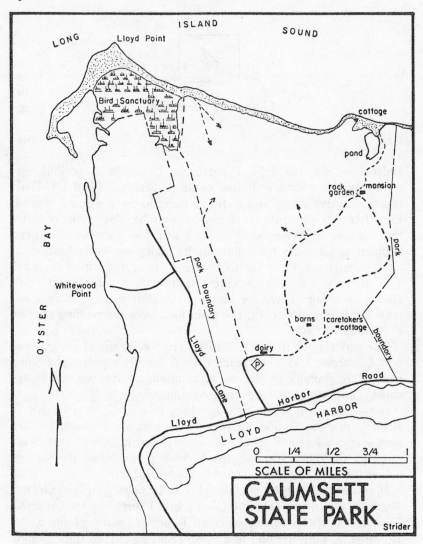

where on Long Island during the warmer months. If you use insect repellent and avoid tall grass, you will probably not be bothered. To be safe, however, examine yourself carefully after your walk. A familiarity with the appearance of poison ivy is also helpful, as this plant is found in the park.

When you arrive at the entrance booth for the parking area, ask

for the free map of the park. As you begin your walk on the paved
driveway that leads to the mansion, notice the large gray buildings
on your left. Rest rooms and a public telephone are available on the
far side of the complex. These gray buildings housed the dairy opera-
tions on the estate during Mr. Field's residence. Note the bucolic
theme of the weather vane on the roof. In addition to providing for
its own dairy needs, the estate supplied its own meat, vegetables,
water, and electricity.

One third of a mile from the entrance booth, the road forks. If the
sun is hot, you may choose to take the fork that leads straight ahead;
this fork winds through shaded woods and is several degrees cooler
than the other route. Otherwise, take the left fork toward the grassy
meadows. Both forks lead to the mansion and are about equal in
length. The large brick building with a fountain near the junction is
the polo pony barn, which is often mistaken for the mansion itself.

In the summer the meadows behind the barn are alive with the
aerial acrobatics of barn swallows as they catch insects just above the
ground. The flat, expansive terrain lacks any hint of proximity to a
major city. The air is clean; except for the park's pickup trucks, an
exquisite silence prevails. Soon the road nears a wooded area which
in spring is carpeted with daffodils. Rhododendrons signal the approach to the mansion.

The mansion was built around 1925 and is in excellent condition.
Visitors are not allowed in any of its sixty-five rooms, but they may
tour the gardens. Step around to the rear of the building and enjoy a
view, spectacular if the weather is clear, of Long Island Sound and
the Connecticut shoreline eight miles away. The lawn slopes gently
from a stone balustrade toward a fresh-water pond below; this is a
fine spot to stop for a few minutes. You may also want to tour the
formal garden on the west side of the building. Here is a chance to
indulge in a little fantasy and pretend for a few moments that you
are the owner of this estate, with all the servants and services at your
command.

As you walk back from the formal garden toward the mansion,
look for a path that starts just to the left of the end of the stone
balustrade. This is the entrance to a rustic rock garden. The stone
steps here lead down past masses of yew and laurel to the fresh-water
pond.

At the pond you may see turtles basking in the sun. I once
counted nine on a log not much bigger than a shoe. The trail circles

Caumsett Park, Lloyd Neck, Long Island, after photo by Robert Cresko

around the east side of the pond and comes quite suddenly to the beach. One moment you are in a deciduous forest with woodland birds; the next, you are standing on a sandy beach listening to gulls and waves lapping at the shore. Here on the north shore the contrast is more dramatic than it is on the south shore, where one gets a sense of the ocean for miles before actually arriving at the beach.

As you turn west, left, along the beach, you will pass an old cottage. The boulders you see here were carried by glaciers from areas far away.

The variety of their colors and textures invites speculation as to their exact origin. The cliffs which border the beach rise higher toward the west. These cliffs are soft and easily eroded. Climbing them is not advised.

Continue west a half mile to the clay cliffs, easily the most spectacular natural feature of the park. The cliffs tower a hundred feet above the beach and are white to red in color. Water oozes out in places, washing wet clay down and across the beach in intricate patterns. Scoop up some wet clay and feel its fine texture. Let the water run out of it until it is malleable, then shape it with your fingers.

With a little imagination, you can see how clay has provided creative inspiration to artisans through the ages.

West beyond the cliffs is a salt marsh. The area is a bird sanctuary for snowy egrets and an occasional great blue heron. A sandspit stretches into Long Island Sound on the other side of the sanctuary. If you wish to go out and explore it, a boardwalk bridges the softer areas of the marsh. A few specimens of prickly-pear cactus can be seen here.

The return road to the parking lot can be found at the northeast corner of the marsh, at a small parking lot reserved for people with fishing permits. Two roads lead back to the park entrance from here; the road perpendicular to the beach is more direct.

The woods along the road are rich in bird life. Among the species you are likely to see are the rufous-sided towhee, brown thrasher, brown creeper, chipping sparrow, and several varieties of woodpecker. A great gray owl, a rare bird normally found in northern Canada, made ornithological history by appearing in Caumsett Park and its environs during January and February of 1979. The red fox is also said to inhabit this area. By walking quietly, you will greatly increase your chances of seeing wildlife.

Continue south until the dairy complex appears on your left. The parking lot lies just beyond the complex.

Now that you have walked the circumference of the park, the many trails that wind through the center of Caumsett Park await you. Or consider exploring the nearby Target Rock National Refuge.

Target Rock, which, like Caumsett, occupies a former estate, lies two miles east of Caumsett on Lloyd Harbor Road. The name is derived from a fourteen-foot boulder that rests on the beach. The rock reportedly served as a target for British gunnery practice during the Revolutionary War. Admission is free, but a permit must be obtained in advance from the Refuge Manager, Target Rock Road, Lloyd Neck, Huntington, NY 11743, or phone (516) 271-2409.

In terms of wildlife, plant life, and terrain, the refuge is a smaller version of Caumsett. Foot trails wind through the refuge. The best times to visit are the spring, when the formal azalea gardens are in bloom; and the winter, when rafts of waterfowl wait on Huntington Bay for warmer weather, sometimes in such great numbers that the floating ducks appear to form a solid black cover.

—ROBERT CRESKO

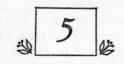

Muttontown Preserve

A bobwhite calls. Then the woods are still. Shadowy sunlight filters through larches and towering white pines, whose castoff needles lie deep underfoot.

Is this where Robert Frost stopped by woods north of Boston? Or where Hemingway played as a boy on the Upper Michigan Peninsula? No, it is the Muttontown Preserve, between East Norwich and Muttontown in Nassau County, twelve road miles from the Queens County line.

The Muttontown Preserve is 600 acres of fields and woodlands, with two-and-a-half miles of marked walking trails. These paths are indicated by color-coded posts set in the ground, including a numbered, self-guiding walk in one section. This walk follows the marked paths and provides about an hour of steady walking. There are also over seven miles of easily followed primary trails and another seven miles of sometimes overgrown secondary trails.

The general public may enter without residential permit or fee to ramble these trails from 9:30 A.M. to 4:30 P.M. seven days a week. Some of the trails are also used by local horseback riders. The preserve is a facility of the Nassau County Department of Recreation and Parks; the phone number of the preserve office is (516) 922-3123.

The motorist who drives from the direction of New York City will reach the preserve 30 miles from the George Washington Bridge. Use Exit 41N from the Long Island Expressway or Exit 35N from the Northern State Parkway. Here Route 106 (Jericho–Oyster Bay Road) goes north 4.3 miles to Route 25A (North Hempstead Turnpike). Be sure to stay right at the fork on Route 106 at 0.8 miles past the expressway. Soon after the railroad tracks, the undeveloped ex-

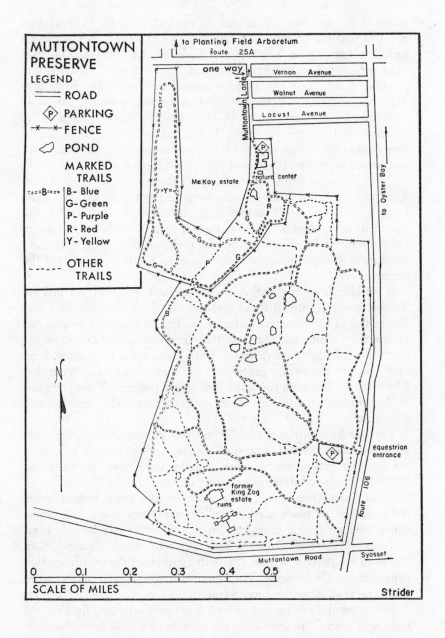

MUTTONTOWN
PRESERVE

LEGEND

═══ ROAD

Ⓟ PARKING

×—×— FENCE

⬭ POND

MARKED
TRAILS

B — Blue
G — Green
P — Purple
R — Red
Y — Yellow

----- OTHER
TRAILS

to Planting Field Arboretum
Route 25A

one way

Vernon Avenue

Walnut Avenue

Locust Avenue

Muttontown Lane

McKay estate

nature center

to Oyster Bay

equestrian
entrance

Route 106

former
King Zog
estate
ruins

Muttontown Road

Syosset

N

0   0.1   0.2   0.3   0.4   0.5
SCALE OF MILES

Strider

panse of the preserve will be seen on the left. Look for Walnut Avenue just past the preserve and turn left (west) onto it. A block later, turn left (south) on Muttontown Lane to the preserve. The turn onto Walnut Avenue comes up just before Route 25A. Anyone reaching Route 25A should turn around and make the turn onto Walnut Avenue (or Vernon Avenue or Locust Avenue). Continue west for a block, then turn south (left) on Muttontown Lane to the entrance to the preserve, which is marked by a sign. A small and sometimes crowded parking lot is located on the east side of the road just before the nature center and the start of the trails.

Public transportation is available. The experienced walker can walk and the less ambitious can complete the trip by taxi from the Long Island Rail Road station in Syosset. The Syosset Taxi Company can be reached at (516) 921-2141. Arrange with the cab driver for the return trip; or phone from the preserve office, if open, or from the nearby Howard Johnson's restaurant on Route 25A north of the preserve.

If walking from the station to the preserve, go north on Jackson Avenue to Muttontown Road and then head west on the road past Route 106 to the preserve. Enter at the first equestrian gate past the intersection, a mile and three quarters from the Syosset depot, on the north side of Muttontown Road. From here, using a compass, head north toward the nature center and the start of the walk. Note that Muttontown Road, on the south side of the preserve, is not the same as Muttontown Lane, the short street between the perserve and Route 25A.

The northwestern part of Muttontown Preserve, where this walk is, is level and wooded. The trails are marked with posts in various colors. The nature center offers a self-guiding map to the trails, which have lettered stations for nature observation.

From the nature center, walk south on the green trail, a broad path marked by posts, past a shallow man-made pond that sometimes dries up during droughts. Frogs and turtles can be seen here, and the preserve staff claims to have seen red-backed salamanders. In less than a quarter of a mile, the path approaches the iron fence that runs through the preserve. Turn here to the right, still on the green trail. You are now walking southwest.

Past a brook bed, the green trail skirts an overgrown field on the right and reaches an intersection a quarter of a mile from the start-

Muttontown Preserve

ing point. Turn right and for five hundred feet follow the green trail as it meanders along the west side of the field. Soon a post shows that the path has become a purple trail. Don't continue, but make an abrupt turn along the trail to the right that goes down a short slope and up to another fence. This is the continuation of the green trail, which veers left from the fence and into a thicket. The path parallels the fence, with the well-manicured arboretum of the McKay estate on the other side.

Soon the fence and then the trail turn north. Here the trail enters the cool and quiet stand of eastern white pine and larch so evocative of Hemingway and Robert Frost. At a fallen tree trunk polished by time and resting walkers, a post indicates a yellow trail leading west; this is a short cut. For the full walk, stay on the green trail. Avoid the shiny leaves of poison ivy and enjoy a soft, fragrant passage on a floor of pine needles. Watch for chickadees and grosbeaks, here to feed on the cone seeds.

Three quarters of a mile from the starting point, the trail nears Route 25A. It curves west and uphill to overlook the road, then continues around to the south. In a quarter of a mile it passes a yellow-blazed post, the other end of the loop cutoff that began near the polished tree trunk. Watch now for a second yellow-marked post a few feet farther down the green trail. Follow the yellow trail here

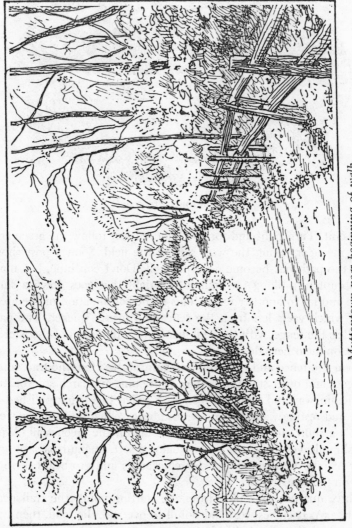

Muttontown near beginning of walk

along a heavily wooded short cut. When you meet the green trail again, follow it along the boundary fence, where bobwhites and their chicks have been seen.

You are now in a section of the preserve that horseback riders like to use, so be ready to step aside. Soon there is an opening in the preserve fence. This leads to many interesting but mostly unmarked trails in the larger part of the preserve to the south of the fence. To the left a purple trail leads back in the direction of the parking lot.

Continue on the green trail, going east about two hundred feet to a left turn in the green trail. Listen for the croak of pheasants in the fields and look for warblers feeding on berries in shrubs and saplings. Before long you pass a familiar brook bed and can turn left on the final as well as the first leg of the circuit, past the man-made pond to the nature center for a round trip of a little more than a mile and a half.

The land of the preserve, including a large section south of Muttontown Road that is closed to walkers, was purchased by the county from the estate of Landsell Christie, with smaller parcels coming from Mrs. Paul Hammond and Mrs. Alexandra McKay. The 50-acre parcel containing the nature walk was a donation of Mrs. McKay, whose mansion and elegantly landscaped estate are visible behind the fence from the green trail. At the urging of the Long Island Chapter of the Nature Conservancy, the Nassau Department of Recreation and Parks in March 1970 opened this section to the public.

After you've taken the circuit of marked trails, you may want to explore further. The section south of the fence consists of fields, with rolling hills to the south. Originally the area was farmed, as nearby land still is. The open fields and the water pipes, troughs, and farm implements still in evidence bear testimony to the land's former use. A dairy farm was active here in the early 1920s. Before then, sheep were raised; local people say that Muttontown got its name from the sheep that farmers herded from here to Syosset.

This section of the preserve contains the now vandalized house reputedly once owned by the exiled king of Albania. Ahmed Bey Zogu, who ruled as King Zog from 1928 to 1946, was driven from his country by Mussolini in 1939 and died in Cannes, France, in 1961. Whether or not he owned the property, it is known that he never occupied it. Nassau County apparently received the property by tax default. Steps, garden walls, and gazebos remain.

In the northeastern corner of the preserve is a short, steep climb up High Point. High Point is a glacial kame, or mound, some fifty feet above the surrounding fields. Unfortunately its significance is geologic rather than scenic; the view from the top is blocked by heavy foliage. Nearby, a kettle pond is the site of the only persimmon trees in the preserve. The woodlands generally are dominated by oak, black birch, and Norway spruce, with thickets of blueberry, maple-leaf viburnum, brier, and mountain laurel. Hawks, owls, woodpeckers, raccoons, opossums, rabbits, and foxes reside here throughout the year.

This section of the park is particularly rewarding for the non-directed walker. Rather than setting up a strict itinerary of sights and stops, the walker visitor can stroll, ready to change course should a tempting goal present itself. It is possible to wander off course in the preserve but difficult to get truly lost, since walking in any direction brings one before long to the wire fence on the perimeter.

The preserve is uncrowded at all seasons, except when school children on organized outings visit the nature center on weekdays or when Boy Scout troops are camping in the fields. Parking can sometimes be difficult, but spaces usually open up before too long. Littering, picnicking, and flora gathering are prohibited; a ranger patrols the trails on horseback to enforce the rules and assist walkers. Picnickers are allowed to use the lawn behind the nature center, where there are toilet and waste-disposal facilities.

The preserve hosts other activities besides walking. In winter, cross-country skiing has been permitted; a ski shop just outside the entrance, on Route 25A across from the Howard Johnson's restaurant, rents touring skis and equipment. A member club of the New York/New Jersey Trail Conference, the Nassau Hiking and Outdoor Club, schedules events here in orienteering; orienteering is a form of cross-country time trial that tests endurance and map and compass skills.

The most popular activity in the preserve is bird watching. The quiet here attracts a variety of species. The ranger is a good person to ask where birds can be observed. The sightings of the past are listed by month inside the nature center. This small area annually hosts over a hundred and fifty species of birds.

—HOWARD PIERSON

NEW YORK CITY: Finding the Oasis

New York City sits at the center of one of the world's great public transportation networks. Anyone living near a subway, anyone who can get to a train or bus line leading to the terminals of Manhattan, can get to the outdoors. The private car, whether owned, borrowed, or rented, may be desirable, but it is not essential.

Attractive walking areas are convenient to the local bus and subway. Manhattan's festive Riverside Park is a short bus or subway ride away for millions of people. In the Bronx, the woods of Pelham Bay Park and Van Cortlandt Park invite many explorations. Alley Park in Queens offers a unique educational environment to families, and Jamaica Bay's wildlife refuge is noted for the richness of its bird life. The hills of Staten Island offer miles of trails; the trip by public transport can be lengthy, but it includes the spectacular ferry ride across New York Harbor.

The train and interurban bus are more expensive and less convenient than local transportation, but they are more comfortable and speedier; and they literally open up the outdoor world in every direction to the day walker.

The beaches, sandy hills, and marshes east and south of the city are reached from Penn Station, at 33rd Street and Seventh Avenue. This terminal is served by the West Side IRT and IND subways, and the BMT subway is only a short distance away. Long Island Rail Road trains offer access to the walking areas of Long Island, but in many cases a cab is required to complete the trip, which can make Long Island an expensive proposition for walkers using the train. Trains on the North Jersey Coast Line leave Penn Station (and Newark) for points along the Jersey shore, including Cheesequake and Sandy Hook; again, the cab is usually necessary to complete the trip.

Trips to the river valleys and rocky ridges of Westchester usually start from Grand Central Station, at Park Avenue and 42nd Street. This station is reached from the East Side IRT and from the Times

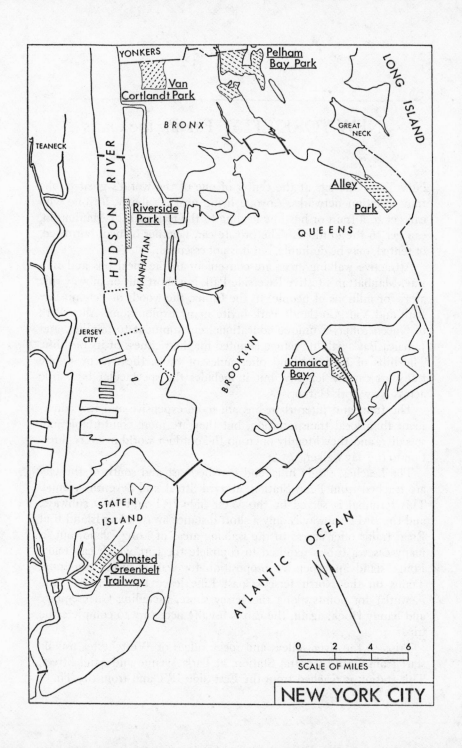

YONKERS

Pelham
Bay Park

LONG
ISLAND

Van
Cortlandt Park

BRONX

GREAT
NECK

TEANECK

HUDSON RIVER

Alley

Riverside
Park

Park

MANHATTAN

QUEENS

JERSEY
CITY

Brooklyn

Jamaica
Bay

STATEN

ISLAND

ATLANTIC
OCEAN

Olmsted
Greenbelt
Trailway

N

0   2   4   6
SCALE OF MILES

NEW YORK CITY

Square shuttle. The Bronx River trail, as well as walks in the lake region around North Castle, are served by the Harlem Division. The Hudson Division, familiar to generations of walkers, serves the Croton Aqueduct stations and Blue Mountain Reservation, and also passes numerous smaller preserves along the Hudson and the challenging trails of the Breakneck Ridge area south of Beacon. The train ride along the Hudson is a feature in its own right, especially after a long walk.

The Ramapos, Hudson Highlands, Watchungs, and all the varied topography west of the Hudson are reached by bus.

Walks northwest of the city usually begin at the George Washington Bridge Station, at 178th Street and Broadway. This station is convenient to the IND A train (175th Street stop) and IRT West Side local (181st Street and walk south and west a couple of blocks). From the station, Red & Tan Lines buses go to the Palisades and Hook Mountain. A Mohawk bus along Route 9W serves the trailheads along the Hudson that lead into Harriman and Bear Mountain parks.

Bus lines fan out across New Jersey and up into New York's Rockland County from the Port Authority Bus Terminal, on Eighth Avenue between 40th and 42nd streets, a block west of the many subways at Times Square. The Short Line route up Highway 17 serves all the trailheads along the western side of Harriman Park, including the Sloatsburg and Tuxedo Park walks. Warwick buses serve Ramapo Mountain State Forest from the Pompton Lakes stop and the southern Wyanokies from the Doty Road stop in Haskell, as well as the trails around Greenwood Lake and, at Mt. Peter, the Appalachian Trail. These buses are popular: on sunny weekends, expect long boarding lines of fellow walkers at the terminals. Other Port Authority buses head southwest to the Watchung Reservation, South Mountain Reservation nearby, and the Delaware and Raritan Canal at Kingston.

To the day walker, the bus possibilities are the most interesting and the most frustrating. It takes time to learn all the routes and to keep up with routing and schedule changes. *Day Walker* gives as much information as possible without being so specific that the book will be out of date the instant it appears. The urban walker can employ several stratagems to supplement the information here. Read county maps such as those put out by Hagstrom, paying special attention to the red lines that indicate bus routes. Use waiting time in terminals to find out what buses serve those routes and collect the current schedules for these routes. Maintain a personal file of up-to-date train and bus schedules. Keep an eye out for notices of service changes in local newspapers and in the *Trail Walker,* and send the *Trail Walker* such news if it hasn't yet appeared there.

In these ways will we find the oasis. Traditionally harried urbanites will never love the weekday commute, but at least the same bus, train, and subway that takes us to work will also carry us away to the woods, fields, and rivers that surround our city.

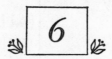

6

Alley Park and Alley Pond Environmental Center

Alley Park in Queens is located in what once was a marsh teeming with wildlife. Matinecock Indians lived in the nearby woods and came down to the shore of Little Neck Bay for fish and shellfish. Even in the 1930s a colonial gristmill still stood on the banks of Alley Pond. Then came the highways. The pond was filled in and the marsh sliced up by the Long Island Expressway and the Cross Island Parkway. The remains of the marsh became a dumping place for refuse and rusting automobile bodies.

Two local residents, Joan and Hy Rosner, were concerned about the destruction of the wetlands and began to discuss the problem with neighbors. Soon a small nature center was established in the park. City officials and school administrators became convinced of the need to preserve what was left and to create a demonstration project on the role of wetlands. The small nature center was superseded in 1976 by the Alley Pond Environmental Center (APEC), which runs demonstration projects and workshops on bird watching, photography, orienteering (a map and compass exercise), and nature study. In the wetlands around the center and in a wooded area a short distance away, the center has set up a network of trails.

The park and APEC are located on the south side of Northern Boulevard in Little Neck, Queens, on the outskirts of New York City 15 miles east of the George Washington Bridge. To get there by car, leave the Cross Island Parkway at Northern Boulevard. The center is a few hundred yards east of the intersection. By subway, take the No. 7 Flushing IRT train to Main Street-Flushing, the last stop. Then board the Q 12 bus from the stop in front of the department store on Main Street and Roosevelt Avenue. The bus goes east on Northern Boulevard; leave it at the first stop after the Cross Island overpass. APEC is just a few feet from the stop. By railroad,

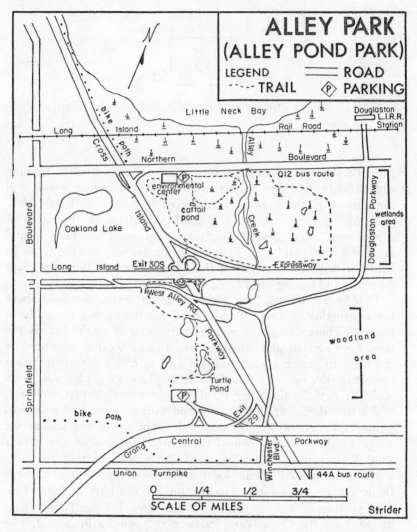

ALLEY PARK
(ALLEY POND PARK)
LEGEND   ROAD
----- TRAIL   Ⓟ PARKING

walk from the Douglaston station on the Long Island Rail Road south to Northern Boulevard and west on Northern Boulevard to the center. A bicycle path along the Cross Island Parkway also leads to APEC.

The basic topography of the area is glacial. During the last ice age, a huge ice sheet pushed ahead of it the dirt and boulders that were to create Long Island. The first plants after the glacial retreat were subarctic species and evergreens. As the climate warmed, these were replaced in gradual stages by the present flora and fauna. The heritage of the glacial age persists in the form of the land. The uplands to the west and south of the center are the dirt and rocks pushed by the glacier, a feature called a moraine.

The simplest trail in the wetlands area of Alley Park is the Cattail Pond Trail near the center. The trailhead is located on the east side of the APEC parking lot. This quarter-mile walk leads south to a platform overlooking a cattail marsh that becomes a pond in the wet season. The trail then swings east to a view over Alley Creek. Soon after it comes to a sitting area, just before returning to the center.

A longer trail, the Pitobek Trail, runs from APEC south to the bridge that takes the Long Island Expressway over Alley Creek. The beginning of the path is well defined by a covering of cedar chips. From the trailhead on the west side of the APEC parking lot, it is about two miles long and takes about an hour to walk. The path follows the edge of the marsh. If you are quiet, you will be able to observe the wildlife. The park is on the Atlantic flyway, and the marshes are popular stopping places for migrating ducks and geese. At various times fifty-two species of birds have been sighted here. Opossums, raccoons, rabbits, turtles, and even an occasional fox have been sighted. Bring binoculars, or rent them at the center.

The wetland trails are often muddy, so hiking boots or rubber boots are suggested. In rainy weather you may also wish to have a spare pair of sneakers along, so that you can change into something dry after the walk. The marsh area has very little shade or shelter, so a hat is advisable. You will probably also need insect repellent.

The woodland area lies to the south of the wetlands area and on the other side of the Cross Island Expressway. To get there from the marsh area, walk south on the Pitobek Trail to the Long Island-Cross Island Expressway interchange. Cross the interchange ramps and follow an overgrown bicycle path under the Long Island Expressway. This path loops up and over the Cross Island, using a pedestrian walkway on the Long Island Expressway bridge. Continue along the path across another highway ramp to the traffic light directly ahead. The woodland area is on the left across the street. A path from this corner leads south through the woods to Turtle Pond.

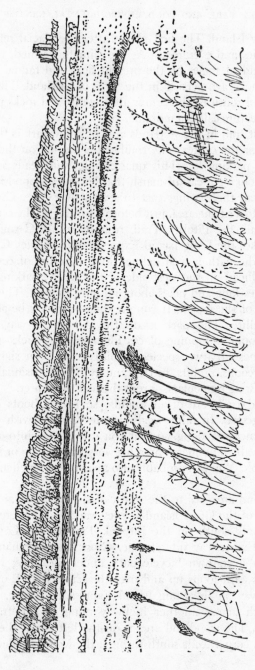

Alley Park, northeast corner looking toward Douglaston

To get to the woodland area from most other parts of the city, take the IND E or F train to Union Turnpike-Queens Boulevard. Take the 44A bus (either the 260th Street or City Line destination) on Union Turnpike going east. Get off at Winchester Boulevard. Walk north (uphill) on Winchester past the tennis court parking area and under the Grand Central Parkway overpass. Directly under this overpass, turn left up the car ramp to the park's upper parking lot. The short Turtle Pond Trail begins on the north side of the lot. Drivers can take the Alley Park exit off the Grand Central Parkway to this same lot.

The Turtle Pond Trail in the woodland area is a self-guided walk around a pond that is shaped like a turtle's head and body. Here you may encounter a blue heron or a red-winged blackbird. In autumn the foliage provides a colorful frame for the migrating birds.

As you begin this walk, notice the small boulders in the woods to the right of the field. These are "erratics," boulders carried from far away by advancing glaciers. Long Island is made up of innumerable boulders like these.

When you reach Turtle Pond you can walk up to its edge, which may be slippery because of mud and wet leaves. The surface of the pond is covered with tiny floating duckweed. Toads, frogs, and turtles live here. Nearby is an area burned over by an arsonist's fire in 1977. Note the succession of plants; as this was written, two years after the fire, the area was almost overgrown with colonizing plants.

To appreciate animal activity here, return at dawn or dusk. At the last few stations on the guided walk, you will hear the rumble of frogs, birdsong, the scratching of crickets.

Trail guides to the self-guided walk at Turtle Pond can be bought and binoculars rented at the Alley Pond Environmental Center, which is open to visitors from 1 P.M. to 4 P.M. every weekday except Wednesdays. On weekends it is open from 11 A.M. to 4 P.M. The rules prohibit camping, fires, firearms, unleashed pets, and alcoholic beverages except beer and ale.

Besides the trail walks, the center hosts other programs and activities, including a recycling center, a solar-heated water system, and an organic garden. To find out what the recycling center will accept and for a newsletter on the latest events, call APEC at (212) 229-4000, or write to them at APEC, 228-06 Northern Boulevard, Little Neck, NY 11363.

The organic garden was begun in the summer of 1978 with the help of Youth Conservation Corps enrollees. It contains a worm farm and a compost pile. All fertilization is done organically—composting, manuring, and cover cropping. Naturally derived supplements such as limestone and peat moss are used. To pollinate the crops, honey bees are raised. Only a small amount of honey is harvested, because the bee colony needs most of it to get through the winter. Visitors are invited into the garden to see the wildflowers, herbs, vegetables, and shrubs and to relax in the sitting area.

The center is particularly well set up for children. Not only are the walks short, but the center also conducts nature-craft demonstrations and holds storybook hours. The center has several types of animals that the children can watch and sometimes touch and hold. Teachers with classes should contact the center for further details; a typical program will consist of an indoor orientation, a discovery walk on the trails, and hands-on activities and time in the natural science area. APEC also has an Outreach Program which can come to the school.

If you particularly enjoy the APEC, you may want to volunteer to work there. Volunteers are the backbone of the center, and they are supported by six staff members, including a naturalist, a fund raiser, and environmental and geological educators. Volunteer application forms are available at the APEC. Whether or not you end up volunteering, the Alley Pond Environmental Center has many things to offer the nature student, environmental activist, bird watcher, parent, child, or the person who simply wants to be outdoors and walk.

—MARA GITLIN

Jamaica Bay

Hiking in the New York area is very much like living in the New York area: diverse backgrounds and traditions persevere and survive next door to one another, each adding to the unique cosmopolitan brew. It's not surprising, then, that Jamaica Bay Wildlife Refuge is flanked by John F. Kennedy International Airport and served by a subway line. Like most New York neighbors, they have learned to get along most of the time.

Approximately fifty thousand people annually visit this unit of the Gateway National Recreation Area, a new federal park put together in the 1970s to provide urban recreation in the New York metropolitan area. Serious bird watchers come to the refuge to spot some of the 312 species that have been sighted here to date; but the majority of the visitors are here to learn about nature and spend a couple of hours outdoors on the two miles of trails leading from the visitors' center.

Jamaica Bay Wildlife Refuge straddles Cross Bay Boulevard in Howard Beach, Queens. It is accessible by car, bus, and subway. The refuge is about 25 miles from the George Washington Bridge. Take the Belt Parkway to Cross Bay Boulevard, turn south, cross the North Channel Bridge, and watch for the refuge entrance. From the Long Island Expressway, take Woodhaven Boulevard (which becomes Cross Bay Boulevard) south to the refuge. Note that driving to Jamaica Bay in summer can be taxing; the boulevard is a major access road to the Rockaways, so weekend beach crowds often jam the route.

By subway, take the IND A or E train to Broad Channel station and walk one mile north to the refuge. The Q21 and Q21A buses also pass the refuge.

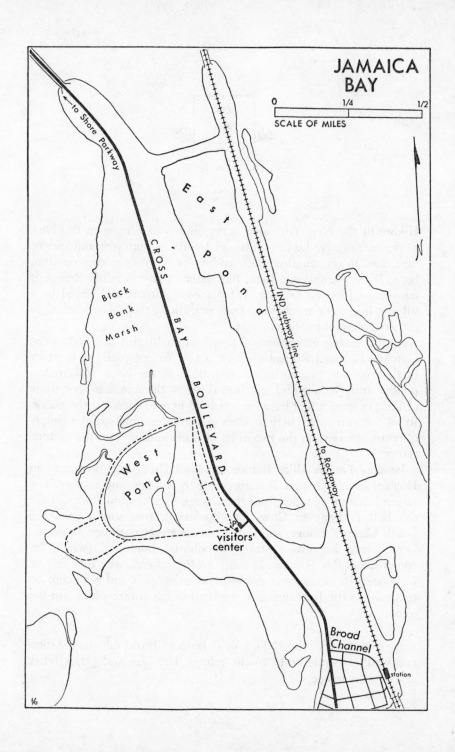

JAMAICA
BAY

0   1/4   1/2
SCALE OF MILES

N

East
Pond

Black
Bank
Marsh

CROSS BAY BOULEVARD

IND subway line

to Shore Parkway

West
Pond

visitors'
center

to Rockaway

Broad
Channel

station

⅛

The subway ride is interesting in its own right, as it crosses the wide expanse of the bay. This is the only subway line in the system that crosses a large body of water. Built in 1877 as a branch of the Long Island Rail Road, the line was acquired in 1952 and rebuilt by New York City after a severe fire destroyed a long section of the trestle in 1950 and the railroad decided to abandon it.

Although the refuge straddles Cross Bay Boulevard, at present only an area on the west side of the boulevard will be of interest to most walkers. Here, a 1.7-mile gravel trail from the visitors' center circles the West Pond. East of the boulevard is the section of the refuge sometimes known as the "wild area," which has no trail, only a path.

No extensive preparations are necessary for a hike in the refuge. The trail around West Pond is circular, level, and clear, with no possibility of getting lost. Sturdy shoes are advisable because of the gravel underfoot. Should you choose to explore the eastern side of the refuge, and it is open, insect repellent is advisable. The tall *Phragmites* reeds harbor lonely insects which enthusiastically welcome the occasional visitor.

First-time visitors to the refuge will need a pass. Fill out the application for a temporary one-day pass at the visitors' center. On the second visit, the temporary pass is surrendered for a permanent one. Holders of the permanent pass are also put on the refuge's mailing list and are kept advised of coming events. The refuge is open on weekdays except Christmas from 8 A.M. to 5:30 P.M., and on weekends from 7 A.M. to 7 P.M. No camping or pets are allowed in the refuge; picnicking is allowed only in a small area near the visitors' center.

Groups of school children, senior citizens, and handicapped persons are welcome at the Jamaica Bay Wildlife Refuge. A group with a reservation will be given a slide-show presentation and a guided tour of the area. The group leader is required to attend an environmental education workshop prior to the group's visit. Slide shows and tours for the general public are given on weekends at 11 A.M., 1 P.M., and 3 P.M. The phone number at the refuge is (212) 474-0613.

Fall is the best time to visit Jamaica Bay. Both the foliage and the wildlife put on their brightest show. Autumn olive brings forth pink berries, and the pokeweeds turn deep purple. Migrating birds descend on the refuge in great numbers as they make their way south

on a timeless path. Binoculars are necessary for effective bird
watching.

How the refuge was created is an example of urban development
in reverse. Land originally inhabited only by squatters was slated to
be developed into an urban recreation complex of beaches and buildings, but instead it became a sanctuary to snowy egrets and glossy
ibises.

In 1938 the lands that were to become the Jamaica Bay Wildlife
Refuge were a contested property. The New York City sanitation
commissioner saw the area as a future dumping site for a burgeoning
waste problem. The city's parks commissioner, Robert Moses, had
other ideas. He viewed the area as a recreation site with "six new
sparkling white beaches and green-shaded waterfront parks." Moses
took his dream to the public in a brochure that juxtaposed two possibilities: a steaming garbage heap, or sailing craft skimming blue
waters.

Moses' campaign began successfully. State legislation transferred
Jamaica Bay to his Parks Department. But then the dream turned
sour. Jamaica Bay turned out to be polluted—too polluted for
beaches and swimmers. So the plans waited while work to clean up
the bay began. There matters rested until a happy accident inter-
vened that led to the creation of the wildlife refuge.

When New York City bought the fire-ravaged Long Island Rail
Road trestle across the bay, it planned to dredge out mud and replace the burned part of the trestle with an embankment. Now
Commissioner Moses re-entered the picture. In return for dredging
rights, Moses obliged the city to create two fresh-water ponds within
the as yet undeveloped recreation area. These two ponds, West Pond
and East Pond, soon began to attract waterfowl and shore birds and
are the heart of today's refuge.

At about the same time, a nesting area for birds was built on
Canarsie Pol, another island in Jamaica Bay. Moses managed to get
sewage sludge piped to the barren island, which provided a base for
the planting of beach grass and plants.

These projects completed the basic construction of the refuge, and
in 1953 it became the Jamaica Bay Wildlife Refuge. But if it took
Robert Moses to establish the refuge through municipal manipu-
lation, it took another man to create the landscape we see today:
Herbert Johnson of the New York City Parks Department.

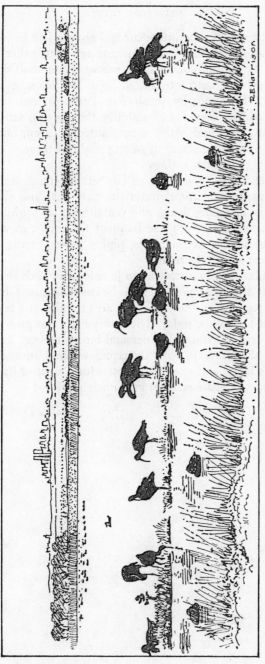

Jamaica Bay Wildlife Refuge, glossy ibises and ducks, after photo by Robert Cresko

Appointed resident superintendent and given a free hand by Commissioner Moses, Johnson gathered cuttings from other locations. Plants such as autumn olive, *Rosa rugosa*, *Rosa multiflora*, pokeweed, and bayberry were introduced. Seeds for Japanese black pine were brought from nearby Jacob Riis Park. Johnson introduced beach grass to "tie down" and stabilize the shifting sands. Grains such as wheat, oats, and barley were planted. Johnson hoped to attract and feed shore birds and migrating wildfowl through a policy of systematic and planned plantings.

And attract birds it did. Jamaica Bay sits on the Atlantic flyway, one of the major migration routes for waterfowl and shore birds. Ducks such as baldpate, scaup, and pintail stop off during their migration. Canada and snow geese frequent the refuge as well. Shore birds such as herons, herring gulls, piping plovers, terns, and even phalaropes nest within the refuge.

Johnson succeeded in attracting to Jamaica Bay birds that had not been seen in the metropolitan area for many years. Glossy ibises hadn't been reported in the New York area for almost a century, but they breed at the refuge today. The snowy egret was pronounced extirpated in 1923, a victim of the demand for its feathers. Today, with SSTs in the sky above it, with thousands walking annually nearby, with millions living and working almost within sight of its nests, the snowy egret is once again resident in our neighborhood.

—Paul D. Czajkowski

Olmsted Greenbelt Trailway

Much of this walk leads over hills, through forests, and around ponds and wetlands. This natural right of way was once intended by highway planners to be a six-lane concrete path down the backbone of Staten Island. Now christened the Olmsted Greenbelt Trailway by the environmentalists who fought to save it, the land harbors raccoons, opossums, pheasants, and muskrats, as well as abundant wildflowers and butterflies.

Across this land is a network of trails that winds for more than thirty miles, usually out of sight of houses and roads. Each of the four trails of the network is blazed in its own color—blue, white, red on white, and yellow—marked with two-inch by three-inch paint patches on trees, rocks, and poles. More trails are being planned.

This sampler of the trails is a leisurely ramble of about four miles, a two-hour walk, using parts of the trails that go through High Rock Park Conservation Center, La Tourette Park, and the Richmondtown Restoration. The walk starts and ends at bus stops. The walking is easy—after a rain, the flat sections of Bucks Hollow may have wet spots, but a little puddle jumping should keep feet dry.

To drive from the east to the greenbelt, which is 30 miles south of the George Washington Bridge, cross the Verrazano Bridge and follow the Staten Island Expressway (I-278) to the Richmond *Road* exit. Take Richmond Road south to Richmondtown to the intersection of Richmond Hill Road and Arthur Kill Road. Parking for Richmondtown is nearby, around the corner to the left on Clarke Street. If coming from the west, cross the Goethals or Bayonne bridges to the expressway and take Richmond *Avenue* south. Turn left on Richmond Hill Road and continue to the restoration area. Walk or take the bus north along Richmond Road to Rockland Avenue and the start of the walk.

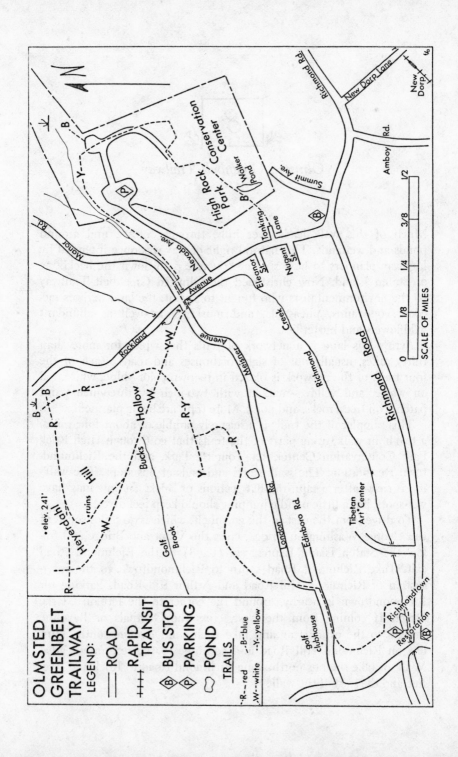

OLMSTED GREENBELT TRAILWAY

LEGEND:

ROAD ▬▬▬
RAPID TRANSIT ┼┼┼┼┼
BUS STOP Ⓑ
PARKING Ⓟ
POND ⬭

TRAILS
R--red   -.-B--blue
W--white   --Y--yellow

High Rock Park
Conservation Center

Walker Pond

Richmond Rd.
New Dorp Lane
New Dorp ⊕ ⅙

Summit Ave.
Amboy Rd.

Tonking Lane
Eleanor St.
Nugent St.

Meisner

Creek

Richmond   Road

Nevada Ave.
Avenue
Rockland   Rd.
Manor Rd.

Avenue

Bucks Hollow
Heyerdahl Hill
•elev. 241'
ruins

Golf Brook

London Rd.
Edinboro Rd.

Tibetan Art Center

golf clubhouse

Richmondtown Restoration

SCALE OF MILES
0   1/8   1/4   3/8   1/2

For most, the trip to the greenbelt will begin with the Staten Island ferry. The Manhattan ferry terminal is convenient to the BMT (Whitehall Street stop) and the East Side and West Side locals of the IRT (South Ferry stop). From 9 A.M. to 9 P.M. at this writing, ferries leave every half hour on Saturdays and Sundays. Weekend service at other times is hourly. The crossing takes twenty-five minutes.

The five-mile ride across New York Harbor costs only twenty-five cents round trip at this writing. Payment is made on the Manhattan side; the return is free. There is much to see on the way. Directly in front of the ferry terminal is Governor's Island, which has its own ferry. The white building at the tip of this island is a ventilating shaft for the Brooklyn-Battery Tunnel. The ship also passes the Statue of Liberty, with the tip of her torch reaching 302 feet above the water.

From the ferry you will notice that Staten Island is much closer to New Jersey than to New York. Legend holds that it became a part of New York because, in a contest, a New Yorker was the first to sail around it in one day.

At the Staten Island ferry terminal in St. George, follow the crowd to the bus concourse and the gate for the No. 113 bus. (The Staten Island Rapid Transit can also be used. The New Dorp station is only a mile from High Rock Park Conservation Center.) The fare is a subway token. Bus drivers do not make change—so be prepared! Ask to be let off at Rockland Avenue, more than a half hour down the island.

To start your walk, turn right on the Rockland Avenue sidewalk. A few hundred yards later, on your right, is Tonking Lane, named for a chicken farmer of some years back. Here you will see your first blazes—blue.

Follow the lane and the blazes past the end of the pavement into High Rock Park and continue up a gentle slope on an ancient roadway. Pass Walker Pond and bear left uphill onto a path, leaving the road. Several short nature trails cut through the park, both blazed and unblazed; pay no attention to the *round* blazes, but continue to follow the *rectangular* blue blazes. The trail swings left across the slope and then right, with park buildings on a higher level to the right. Notice that two blazes together signal that the trail is going to make a sharp turn. In sight of houses (located outside the park), continue up the small hill past a comfort station to the museum and nature center. It's worth a visit inside.

The trail leads along the paved road to the Garden for the Blind, and then loops through two park "laboratories" for school groups before returning to the road. Soon you pass two rain shelters not far from the trail; the fence behind the second one is the boundary of the Moravian Cemetery.

Almost at the bottom of a little hill, the blue trail turns away from the road—*do not follow it*. To the right is a small gravel parking area, with another just down the road; and at the far corner of this first lot are the blazes of a yellow trail.

Descend slightly on the yellow trail to the brook. After a sharp left turn here, zigzag along the left bank on the yellow trail until houses are visible on the left. You are heading for the Rockland Avenue-Manor Road intersection, out of sight on the other side of the bushes. The trail crosses the brook and comes out on Manor Road just before the intersection.

At the traffic light Manor Road crosses Rockland Avenue and becomes Meisner Avenue. A few yards farther on, Meisner Avenue crosses a brook, where the yellow trail enters the woods to the right.

Notice that a white blaze has joined the yellow. Continue on this *white* when the yellow turns away, just after a turn to the left. The red-dot trail crosses here; you will be coming back on this red trail, but for now continue on the wide and straight white-blazed trail. This area is called Bucks Hollow. This oak-beech-tupelo wilderness with swamplets of sumac and rushes is the habitat of opossum, raccoon, and muskrat. Out in the nearby meadows is the cottontail rabbit. Pheasants and, in season, hawks also share the open areas. There are three varieties of sumac, several types of dogwood, quantities of blueberry and blackberry bushes, and a variety of bushes and trees.

When the white trail reaches the large, grassy meadow, walk another sixty paces and leave the trail, following an unmarked path that goes diagonally to the right and up a dirt bluff to a small grove of trees that hides the stone foundations of the Heyerdahl house. This spot is about 240 feet above sea level. The area was once a large fruit farm with an extensive vineyard. The house itself was built around 1860 and burned down around 1910. (If you prefer to stay on the marked trail through the meadow, continue following the white blazes around the shoulder of the hill nearly to the top, and then turn sharp right onto the intersecting red trail.)

From the Heyerdahl ruins, climb on a wide, gradually ascending pathway across the meadow to intersect the red trail at its highest point. From here the view opens in a great arc, with wooded hills in all directions and almost no sign of humanity. In clear weather there are two glimpses of New York Harbor: one through a narrow notch between hills, and the other a wider view across the marshes to the right, with New Jersey's Atlantic Highlands visible in the distance.

The rest of our ramble follows the red-dot trail all the way to Richmondtown, and it's downhill all the way. From the viewpoint go to your right through the meadow and down into the trees. In the trees the red path appears to cross another trail, but actually the two trails each make sharp turns here. Make a right to stay on the red trail.

A few hundred yards and you are back in the thickets of Bucks Hollow again. It's hard to believe this area was once slated to be buried under a highway interchange. In the thicket, watch for the blazes; at the fork, follow them to the right and then cross the white trail. (This is where you were before!) Keep straight on the red trail (here with the yellow) and in about three hundred and fifty yards follow the red off the road and into the woods on the left. (The yellow continues on.) After a zigzag in the forest, enter a tree-girt meadow with the La Tourette golf course visible through the trees to the right. Bear slightly to the right as you cross the meadow and pick up the blazes on the far side.

As you pass a leafy but stagnant pond on the left, the blue trail will join and keep you company. If the foliage is not too thick, look for the Staten Island Lighthouse to your left. The 350,000-candlepower beam is 231 feet above sea level and can be seen for over twenty miles.

The trail eventually follows around to the left and comes out on London Road where the road makes a right-angle bend. Follow the road to the right a short block to Edinboro Road and turn right along that. When the driveway for the golf course's clubhouse angles off to the right (rest rooms and a bar inside the clubhouse are open to the public), skirt the underbrush along the edge of a lawn on the left side of Edinboro Road until the trail, an old road, breaks through the brush. In a small clearing, bear left and descend a steep bluff. The trail crosses a barren-looking cleared area and enters a small grove on a hillock. Here the trail joins a sidewalk through the grove and across Richmond Creek. This is the only stream that begins and ends entirely in the city of New York. Here it widens into John Dunn's Pond, now occupied by ducks, geese, and even a few chickens, who will be quite willing to share your lunch. There is a church parking lot on the other side of the pond. This spot is the end of the red trail and the north edge of the Richmondtown Restoration.

The Richmondtown Restoration is worth a visit in its own right. It has been called a northern Williamsburg. The plan of the Staten Island Historical Society is to establish a permanent slice of the past

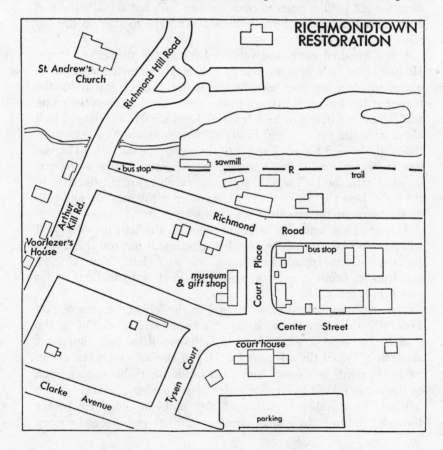

Voorlezer's House, Richmond, after photo by Albert Field

for us to visit. The ambitious program envisions a collection of more than thirty houses dating from colonial days to the turn of the century.

Richmondtown began as a landing for Indian traders coming in the Fresh Kills; it was the hub of the island and the scene of Revolutionary-era skirmishes. For some years it was the county seat. When St. George outgrew and surpassed it, Richmondtown declined.

The oldest building, Voorlezer's House, dates from before 1696; built by the Dutch congregation, it is the oldest schoolhouse still standing in the country and is a National Historic Landmark. Other buildings, of various dates, are the settings for demonstrations of a variety of early crafts and trades. The historical museum occupies an 1848 brick building and is open daily except Monday from 10 A.M. to 5 P.M. (Sundays from 2 P.M. to 5 P.M.). Inside are archaeological relics, costumes, farm utensils—and a gift shop in the form of an old-fashioned store, with real penny candy.

St. Andrew's Church, although in the restoration area, did not have to be moved to its present site; it is a historical building itself, having been founded in 1708 and reconstructed in 1872 after a fire. It was chartered by Queen Anne of Great Britain, who donated a silver chalice and other gifts to the church. The graveyard is the last resting place of several soldiers from the Revolutionary War; the father and grandfather of Mother Elizabeth Seton are also buried here.

The No. 113 bus stop for the return to the ferry is at the foot of Court Place, on Richmond Road.

The four trails of the Olmsted Greenbelt Trailway offer a variety of routes beyond the one sketched here, and all of them end at bus stops for easy access by public transportation. The Greenbelt Circular (blue), La Tourette (yellow), Willow Brook (white), and Richmondtown Circular (red on white) trails were all blazed by Conservation and the Outdoors, an organization founded and led by Tom Yoannou.

The preservation of the Olmsted Trailway is the result of a long and cooperative effort by many conservation groups, including the New York/New Jersey Trail Conference. The monument to their success is the unused interchange on the Staten Island Expressway between the Verrazano Bridge and the Goethals Bridge. From this interchange a major highway was to have led south along the spine

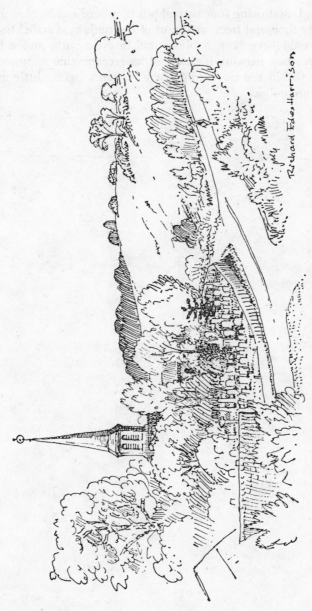

St. Andrew's Church, Richmond, Staten Island

of the island, destroying four natural ponds gouged out by glacial action, twenty thousand trees, and most of the trailway. Parallel to the highway would have been a bridle trail, a cycle path, and a foot trail. Today's trail network is clearly of far greater value in providing us an area within the city limits where we can all get a little away from the automobile.

—ALBERT FIELD

Riverside Park

A walk in Manhattan's Riverside Park should be savored, not hurried. Although this walk is only about three miles in length, there are baseball and basketball games to be watched, river traffic to be reviewed, and juicy franks to be munched. The way is level and paved; much of it runs right along the edge of the Hudson.

Since the walk parallels subway and bus lines, it can be shortened at will. Take the IRT Broadway local to 116th Street. (If coming by car, park near the 72nd Street-Broadway station and take the local north to 116th.) When you come out of the subway, you will be at Columbia University. South of you are the bookstores and eateries around the university. Walk north on Broadway to 120th Street (which is called Reinhold Niebuhr Place on the west side of Broadway). As you walk up Broadway you will see three tall apartment buildings far ahead; these mark the approaches to the George Washington Bridge. Closer is a depression, with heights beyond; this is 125th Street and Harlem Heights.

Turn west (left) on Reinhold Niebuhr Place. Today it is lined with buildings, but two hundred years ago it was a battlefield. After a headlong retreat up Manhattan, Washington's troops made a stand along what is now 120th Street. The British stood about a block south, and the two lines fired at each other until the British finally broke. The battle was one of the first successes that the colonial amateurs had against trained European soldiers.

You will soon reach Riverside Drive, the last street. At your right is Riverside Church, modeled in part after Chartres Cathedral. Just north of you, but almost hidden in summer by the trees, is Grant's Tomb. Open daily from 9 A.M. to 5 P.M., it is the final resting place of the eighteenth President of the United States, Ulysses S. Grant, and his wife, Julia. The mausoleum is maintained by the National

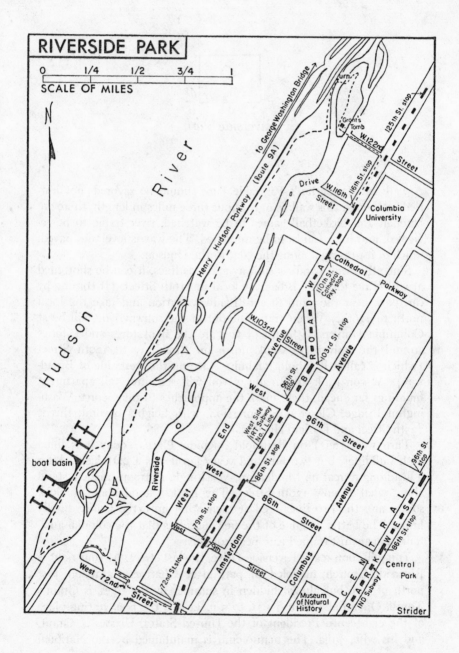

Park Service. Inside the visitor can get a brochure on the history of the tomb. In the side rooms are dioramas depicting Grant's greatest victories as a general in the Civil War.

Riverside Park existed before the construction of the tomb. When the tomb was built in 1897, the park's architect warned that "it will be extremely unfortunate if . . . the remains of the dead are brought into close association with the gayety of the Promenade at this culminating point." His fears that the tomb would be depressing were unfounded: children play baseball on the steps of the mausoleum, and the mausoleum itself is surrounded by colorful, and controversial, free-form benches covered with mosaic patterns.

Walking directly north from Grant's Tomb brings you to the brow of Claremont Hill, some 140 feet above the Hudson, with a view up the river to the George Washington Bridge, five miles north, and the wooded Palisades beyond. Now walk west off the hill, cross Riverside Drive, and head south on the sidewalk. Soon you will come to a quaint and affecting little monument about a hundred yards northwest of the tomb. Just off Riverside Drive a marble urn sits enclosed by a fence at the edge of a steep drop-off. The urn is inscribed: "Erected to the Memory of an Amiable Child." In 1797 a five-year-old boy who lived near here was killed in a fall from these rocks. His father erected the urn. A few years later, forced by business reverses to leave the area, he asked that the monument be preserved. His request has been honored to this day by all the succeeding generations of builders, roadmakers, and developers who have otherwise utterly transformed these heights.

Enter the main part of Riverside Park via the path opposite the end of Reinhold Niebuhr Place (120th Street) and follow the path down, past side paths that diverge left along the slope, to the bottom to the rather eroded stairway. Directly underneath the path in a tunnel are the tracks of a railroad freight line that runs down to freight yards at 72nd Street: note the ventilation gratings set in the ground. To your right are tennis courts with attended rest rooms. (A drawback of a crowded city walk like Riverside Park or the Paterson industrial restoration is that rest rooms are required, a point not soon forgotten by anyone who has been unable to find relief in time of need. One solution is to use rest rooms when available, whether needed or not; another is to know that most restaurants, bars, and churches are tolerant of the visitor who maintains a presentable appearance and passes through quietly.) Beyond the tennis courts the tracks emerge from the tunnel to cross the 125th Street depression on a viaduct. Ahead you can hear, although at this point in summer not see, the six lanes of the Henry Hudson Parkway.

Those who love Riverside Park are concerned that future development of the parkway may damage it. Surprisingly, the park was created by the construction of road projects. The original Riverside Park was developed along with Riverside Drive in the 1870s by Frederick Law Olmsted, famed designer of Central and Prospect parks. His 215-acre park here (including Riverside Drive) landscaped only the hillside to the bottom of the slope; below the slope were the then open railroad tracks, and beyond were the banks of the Hudson, with dumps, decaying barges, squatters' hovels, and junkyards. The smell of cattle cars and the noise of endless switching infuriated local residents, but money was lacking to complete the park.

Finally, in the 1930s, Robert Moses found the money; everything in the park from the base of the slope out to the bulkhead at the river's edge was created by Moses as part of his West Side Improvement. The same project that sliced through Inwood Hill and carved up Van Cortlandt Park added 132 acres to Riverside Park and made it what it is today.

Swing along the path from the tennis courts and you shortly come to a junction, where another path leads up into the trees above you. Here is the first drinking fountain of many, featuring New York City drinking water, which, in this connoisseur's opinion, is better than any spring water this side of the Catskills (assuming, of course, that the fountain is working). Shortly thereafter is the first of several mock battlements overlooking the Hudson. At the second, smaller "battlement," the area below opens up enough to accommodate playing fields, which stretch southward for nearly a mile. Not long thereafter, the path along the top opens unobtrusively into a mall. The mall runs, perfectly straight, almost to 96th Street under a double row of maples. In summer it teems with hot dog vendors, picnickers, bicyclists, joggers, and volleyball players. In the winter, after a snowfall, it is quiet and majestic; cross-country skiers come here to practice.

When the mall ends, the path curves a little to the right, then forks, with the left fork running ahead along a black picket fence and the right fork dipping down to an underpass beneath the highway. Follow the right fork under the arched overpass. (The left fork goes ahead to a shaded, rather noisy playground and then out to Riverside Drive and an intersection with 95th Street.)

As you go under the arch, the great vista of the Hudson opens up.

Far to the north is the George Washington Bridge. Ahead are the Palisades, with apartment buildings on the bluff and factories at the water's edge. Far down the river, on a point jutting out from the Jersey side, is Stevens Institute of Technology, in Hoboken; on the Manhattan side is the boatyard at 79th Street, with the ship piers downriver. Barges, sailboats, and cruisers move past in procession, accompanied in tourist season by the ever present Circle Line ships, as industrious as water skimmers. Overhead, helicopters constantly pass, and far above, the big jets settle into their approach to La Guardia. Surprisingly, the river side of the park is quieter than the slope side; noise seems to evaporate into the enormous spaciousness.

All this land around 96th Street at the river is fill from the Improvement. Once Strykers Bay was here. In 1776, on the day before the Battle of Harlem Heights, three British ships anchored here to harass the colonial retreat. Now, railings run along the top of the breakwater. Grownups and small boys fish from this river's-edge promenade. Small as the area is between the highway and the river, there's room for ten clay tennis courts and two parking lots for sightseers. Walk south past a grove of locusts and sweet gums. Shortly past the second parking lot, the path forks again. One branch accompanies an access road under the parkway; the other goes ahead, soon becoming a dirt path. So few are the places that one can walk along the Hudson that you may prefer to take the dirt path down to the 79th Street boatyard, where the river promenade begins again, but our walk goes back under the highway, up past some interestingly shaped cherry trees, and through an opening in a low, sandstone-colored wall onto the double paths of the long esplanade between 94th and 82nd streets.

This esplanade curves sinuously around the foot of the slope. To your left, almost hidden in the trees, is a large, tree-shaded playground. On the other side of the playground, completely hidden from this spot in summer, is an open bowl of a slope that in winter offers the best sledding of any in this park and perhaps the best in Manhattan. On a bluff overlooking the slope and the esplanade is the circular form of the Soldiers' and Sailors' Monument at 89th

Street. Built in 1900 to commemorate the Union fighting men of the Civil War, it is modeled after the Monument of Lysicrates in Athens.

The benches along the esplanade are much favored by retired people (unlike the section north of 96th Street, which features picnicking families, or the section below 79th, which, on the side of the parkway away from the river, is dotted with sunbathing singles). The views here are limited, but it's a fine feeling to go striding along this open area, with the sun beating down and the city apartments towering off to the left beyond the trees.

After about a quarter mile, a spur trail drops away to the right. This is a short cut down to the 79th Street marina. Soon after is the end of the esplanade, where stonework again curves around to enclose the walk. Immediately behind the stone wall to your right, a stepped path winds down. Before you take it, stop to look around. That rocky knoll in front of you, almost hidden from this angle by the trees, is unofficially called "Mt. Tom." Originally the Soldiers' and Sailors' Monument was built there, and the site has also been proposed for various statuary. So far it is untouched except by spray-paint graffiti. Below and to the right of the knoll is another playground, with attended rest rooms. The ice cream man is usually here at the gate on summer weekdays, and on weekends a hot dog vendor often joins him.

The set of stairs that winds down to the right behind the wall at the end of the esplanade takes you to a small clearing below the wall, where the curious can peer through the window of a (usually) unlocked door to see the enormous railroad tunnel that runs beneath the park. To the left is the underpass beneath the highway, which opens up on the other side to another grand vista. Ornamental cherry trees line the path along the river's edge past the boat basin; try to walk this section at least once in the spring, when the blossoms are spectacular.

The 79th Street boat basin is home to various craft and also to about eighty-five year-round houseboaters. Compared to private marinas, city marinas are rather spartan, but this one offers a special attraction: parking in an underground 200-car garage is included in the dockside rent. That imposing many-tiered structure to your left houses the parking lot, railroad tracks, and a rotunda which in the summer of 1981 was used as a theater.

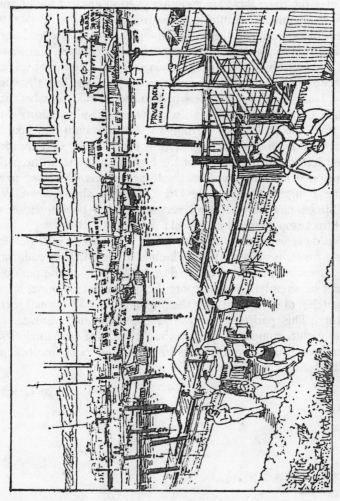

Marina, 79th Street and Riverside Park, after photo by Walter Houck

South of the marina the park widens to include a playground with enormous fountains, several ballfields, and even a small track and field stadium popular with local joggers. Benches line the walk with views over the river; these are good places to sit and eat the hot dogs and ice cream purchased outside the marina gates.

A few blocks south of the marina the park ends. Gates lead out to the waterfront beyond. In the distance is a ruined dock, and beyond that are the docks of the major passenger lines. Often tugboats can be watched from here as they nudge enormous liners into the docks. On the land side the view is less inspiring: a desolate baseball field, and then a jumble of roads on stilts over the railroad switching yards.

To leave the park, circle beyond the little stadium and take the gradual path up to the landing. Here is the last view over the river. To your left, on the other side of the highway, is more of the park— here an open field usually dotted with sunbathers. Continue past a drinking fountain to Riverside Drive. Straight ahead down West 72nd Street, past several small restaurants and bookstores, is the 72nd Street stop (express and local) on the IRT Broadway subway.

Riverside is an urban park, with urban problems. It is proverbially not safe for lone walkers after dark and, at the northern end, sometimes unnerving even during the day. Many areas of the park offer no quiet or serenity. In some spots the grass is totally gone, leaving large patches of bare earth. But the problems are only a small part of the story. This park is a festival: vital, exuberant, diverse. Even Mother Nature somehow bears up: in the midst of everything, West Side cooks sneak to favorite spots to collect the leeks, burdock, and garlic that still grow wild here.

—REYNARD DARGENT

Van Cortlandt Park

Van Cortlandt Park is one of the largest and most varied of New York City's parks. Located in the northwest corner of the Bronx at the Yonkers border, it has many miles of trails, bridle paths, and paved paths.

The park is easily reached by car or public transportation. The northern terminus of the Broadway IRT local at 242nd Street is at the southwest corner of the park. From the station, buses run along Broadway (Route 9) north to Yonkers and beyond. Another local bus line connects the pedestrian overpass crossing the New York State Thruway at the northern end of the park to the last stop of the East Side IRT express on Jerome Avenue at Woodlawn Cemetery.

The Henry Hudson, Sawmill, and Mosholu parkways meet in the park. Just west of this parkway intersection, the Henry Hudson Parkway crosses Broadway. Take the Broadway exit and continue south on Broadway, with the park on the left, until a parking space is found.

Van Cortlandt Park is suitable for short or long strolls. The varied terrain offers plenty of room for a full day's walk. On sunny weekend days the picnic areas will be crowded, but peace and quiet await in the surrounding woods. Along Broadway there are many places to eat. The office building of the Van Cortlandt Park Golf Course (a public facility) has public rest rooms and an indoor snack bar that is open daily, including Sundays, from Memorial Day to Labor Day.

One suggested walk of about three miles starts from the 242nd Street IRT subway station. Enter the park and walk east and then north, with the modernistic buildings of the swimming pool to your right. Ahead will be the Van Cortlandt Mansion. The house and grounds are surrounded by a tall wrought-iron fence. As you pass, note the current visiting hours posted on the signboard near the

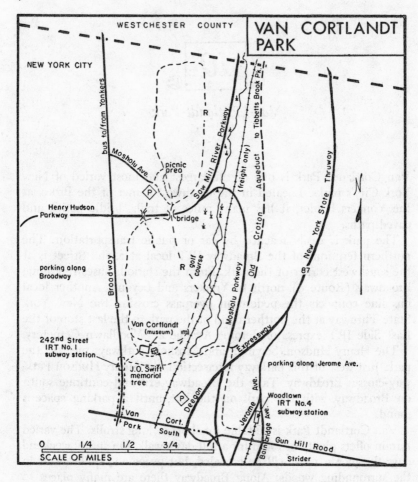

south entrance gate. It is suggested that the walk through the park be taken first, with a visit to the house and grounds at the end of the walk.

Continue past the house to a wide path that circles the parade ground and playing fields. This path turns north toward a rocky ridge, Vault Hill, and runs parallel to the railroad tracks of the old Putnam Division, off in the trees to the right. Passenger trains no longer run along this line, but there is an occasional freight train.

On the ridge are several trails, one marked haphazardly with a red blaze. This is the trail used by the cross-country runners in the track and field events held in the park. Runners use this path at all times, but it's wide and there's lots of room remaining for walkers. The path goes up the ridge at a slant. Off to the left, toward the rocky outcropping that juts up from the playing field, is the Van Cortlandt family burial plot, surrounded by an iron fence, and the family burial vault. In 1776 this vault was the hiding place for the records of New York City under British rule; the city's recording clerk was a Van Cortlandt. The metal chest containing the papers is now in the hall of the Van Cortlandt Mansion.

Go over an iron bridge crossing the Henry Hudson-Saw Mill River Parkway. Follow the red blazes past a picnic area and enter a wooded area. In the woods along this path the occasional picnic tables with benches are suitable for a lunch stop, if you bring your own lunch.

The marked path eventually turns west and then south, back over the bridge crossing the highway. Turn right just after the bridge and swing south to the large field used for ball games. On a sunny Sunday afternoon this open expanse is alive with running, jumping, soccer, volleyball, football, and other activities. Walk along the path that runs south on the west side of the field parallel to Broadway until you reach the Van Cortlandt Mansion.

This Georgian-style house, the oldest building in the Bronx, was built by Frederick Van Cortlandt in 1748 in what had been a cornfield, and was occupied by the Van Cortlandt family until 1889, when it became the property of the Parks Department.

During the Revolutionary War the house was important to both sides. Twice during the war George Washington stayed at the house. The first time was during the campaign that ended in the Battle of White Plains early in the war. Later, in the closing days of the war, Washington and the French commander, Rochambeau, met here to discuss their final military strategy. When the American troops departed for their fateful junction with Lafayette at Yorktown, Washington had campfires kept on Vault Hill to fool the British into thinking the Americans were still north of the city. Finally, in 1783, upon the British evacuation, the triumphal return march of the Americans into New York City began here.

The Van Cortlandt Mansion is now restored to its former elegance. The rooms give an idea of the life of a well-to-do Dutch-English family in the late eighteenth century and are furnished with

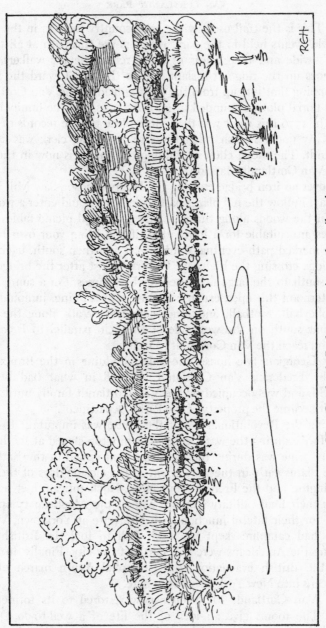

Van Cortlandt Park swamp from the railroad

seventeenth- and eighteenth-century American, Dutch, and English pieces. The basic construction material of the house is rubblestone accented by brick trim around the windows. One unusual touch is the figures placed above the windows. These show the Dutch heritage of the builder, for although rare in America they were a common sight in Holland.

On the grounds of the mansion are an herb garden and an outdoor exhibit consisting of a section of a brick window frame with iron bars. This was once part of a British prison building for American soldiers and others. Close to the front of the house and inside the surrounding fence is a red oak with a memorial plaque set in the ground in front of it. This tree was planted in memory of J. Otis Swift.

J. Otis Swift (1871–1948) was a newspaperman, naturalist, humanitarian, and enthusiastic hiker. For twenty-six years he published a nature feature, "News Outside the Door," which appeared daily in the New York *World*. His articles spoke of the glories of the woodland trails and often referred to the Ancient Order of Yosiah and to its members, the Yosians, on their nature rambles. Swift's first name was Josiah, but the order was merely a figment of his imagination. Soon he began to receive letters and calls from the readers of his column who wanted to join the Yosians on their nature walks. When he invited the public in print to join him on a Sunday walk, fifty persons showed up. At the walk a few weeks later there were hundreds. He founded the Yosian Brotherhood, which was a federation of hiking clubs. In the years that followed the more than thirty subdivisions of the Brotherhood had over 200,000 members. For the rest of his life he led Yosians on weekend hikes in the city parks and in lower Westchester.

Van Cortlandt Park was one of his favorite places. His group would meet at the Van Cortlandt Park subway station, walk through the park, and continue north on the Old Croton Aqueduct trail (see map) beyond the borders of the city to Tibbetts Brook Park. Another of Swift's frequent treks was to the swamp in the center of the park. This, one of the few fresh-water marshes in the city, still exists but is now locked in and reduced in size by Mosholu Parkway, the Saw Mill River Parkway, and the railroad. It is accessible from the lower end of Van Cortlandt Lake by walking north along the railroad track.

Swift wrote of this area: "One of the greatest educational institutions in New York is the great swamp in Van Cortlandt Park. It was designed by the Architect who created George Washington, Abraham Lincoln, the Declaration of Independence and the Emancipation Proclamation; who dictated the First Chapter of Genesis and the Sermon on the Mount. The swamp is almost the only thing left in the city fresh from the hands of its Maker and bearing His finger prints. It inspires love of beauty in the minds of untold thousands who wander there and get their first and lasting impression of the entrancing loveliness of wild Nature from it. It is a greater museum than that at 77th Street and Central Park West; a greater library than that at Fifth Avenue and 42nd Street. It contains more interesting living creatures than there are human beings in the United States. At sunset and sunrise it contains more beautiful and better painted pictures than there are in the Museum of Art. It is a bird, animal, botanical and waterlife sanctuary such as, once destroyed, the city government, in all its glory, could not recreate. To the city's nature lovers, it is a permanent laboratory for the study of wild life."

The memorial tree near Van Cortlandt Mansion was planted by the Parks Department with funds collected by his followers after his death. On the third Sunday in May of every year, those of us who walked with Swift hold a gathering at the tree and once again read his memorial plaque: "We seek Jehovah on the mountain tops and rest our souls in the silence of woodland places."

—NAT LESTER

11

Pelham Bay Park

Pelham Bay Park, in the far northeast corner of the Bronx, offers miles of footpaths through dense woods and along the rocky coast-line of Hunter's Island, near Orchard Beach. This walk is about four miles long. Since Orchard Beach is very crowded during the summer, the best time to take the walk is during the other seasons. Even on the clearest days of spring or fall, the area will be nearly deserted. In winter, a few bird watchers and cross-country skiers may be encoun-tered.

The "Park on the Sound," 10 miles from the George Washington Bridge, can easily be reached by car or public transportation. By car, take the Hutchinson River Parkway to the Orchard Beach exit and follow the signs to the enormous parking lot. By public trans-portation, take the No. 12 bus to the park. The No. 12 bus runs along Fordham Road and Pelham Bay Parkway and connects with all the subways in the Bronx.

Leaving the plaza where the Pelham Bay IRT local line ends, the bus crosses over the New England Thruway and enters the park on the Pelham Bay Parkway. The high mound on the right just before the Pelham Bay Parkway crosses the Hutchinson River is the Talla-poosa landfill. Once an offshore island, the tract is now a vast heap of refuse covered by dirt. The tall buildings on the other side of the parkway are Coop City, a controversy-torn housing development where more than fifty thousand people live. The now lost site of Anne Hutchinson's colony is also somewhere in that direction. Al-most three hundred and fifty years ago, she and her followers fled to the banks of the river, seeking religious freedom. Instead, they in-truded upon the Siwanoy Indians, who repeatedly warned the colo-nists to leave. Finally, their patience exhausted, the Siwanoy attacked and wiped out the small colony in 1643.

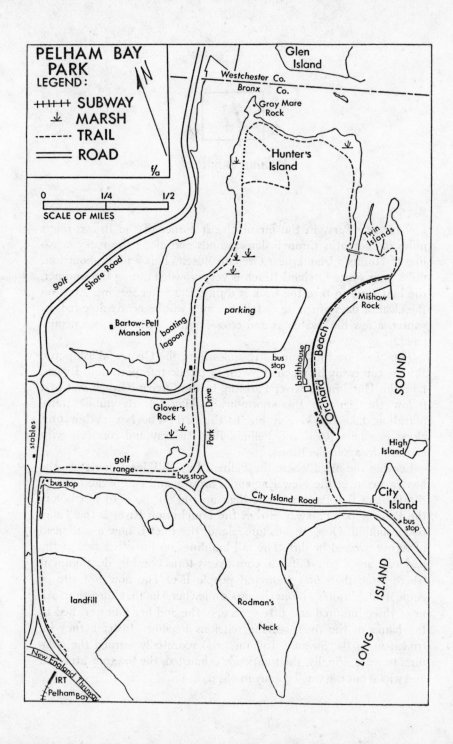

PELHAM BAY
PARK
LEGEND:
┼┼┼┼┼ SUBWAY
↓ MARSH
- - - TRAIL
═══ ROAD

f/a

0   1/4   1/2
SCALE OF MILES

Glen
Island

Westchester Co.
Bronx   Co.

Gray Mare
Rock

Hunter's
Island

Twin
Islands

golf   Shore Road

Mishow
Rock

parking

Bartow-Pell
Mansion

boating
lagoon

bus
stop

bathhouse

SOUND

Orchard Beach

stables

Glover's
Rock

Park Drive

golf
range

High
Island

bus stop

bus stop

City Island Road

City
Island

bus
stop

landfill

Rodman's
Neck

LONG ISLAND

New England Thruway

IRT
Pelham
Bay

As you cross the Hutchinson River bridge, pull the cord to let the driver know you want to leave the bus at the next stop. When the bus turns off the parkway onto City Island Road, get off and cross City Island Road to pick up the sidewalk path on the other side.

Turn right on the path, following it on a low hill above the road. The path leads past a miniature golf course and driving range and then swings north, following the shore of a pond. Don't cross the road when the path does; stay on the east side until the access road to the beach from the Hutchinson comes in from the left. On the hillside a little way up the road are two large rocks. The larger of these has a historical marker attached. This is Glover's Rock, commemorating an American success in the early days of the Revolutionary War. In 1776, when Washington was retreating from New York after the Battle of Harlem Heights, the British landed forces here on Rodman's Neck to cut across Westchester and intercept his march. The redcoat column was bushwhacked by Colonel Glover and 750 Massachusetts patriots, enabling Washington to reach White Plains and make his successful stand there.

Now cross the access road and walk on, staying in the strip between the parking lot and the lagoon. (Car drivers can pick up the walk here.) The lagoon is set up for rowing races. Lanes are marked with large numbers, and the high open concrete judges' stand is soon passed. You may see racing boats practicing, their oars cutting precisely into the water as they skim over the waves.

Visible across the lagoon is the Bartow-Pell Mansion, with its formal gardens. Constructed in 1842, it has been restored and is open to the public. Call (212) 885-1461 for current hours and other details.

Continue along the water past the fishermen and then past a stand of *Phragmites* reeds. On the other side of the reeds, pick up a path leading into the quiet woods of Hunter's Island.

Hunter's Island takes its name from John Hunter, who bought this land in the early nineteenth century, when it was still an island. In 1812 he erected a mansion on the top of the hill. Today the mansion is gone and the northern end of the onetime island is covered with dense woods, crossed by a network of footpaths and old roads. Trails cut through waist-high masses of goldenrod, jewelweed, and reeds. Some of the lesser-used trails become so overgrown at the height of summer that they can't be followed.

The trails and woods are littered, but the wild strawberries and blackberries make up for the inconvenience, especially in July and

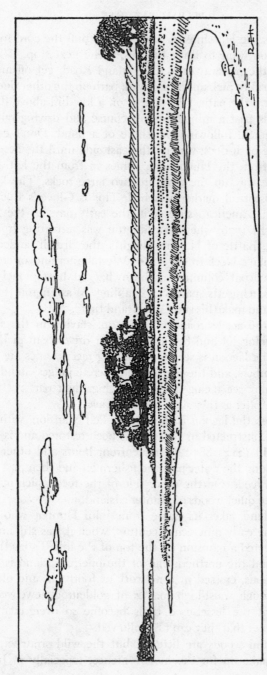

Pelham Bay Park. Long Island Sound from the northeast corner of New York City, after photo by Benjamin Houck

August. In fact the woods are a paradise for food foragers and also, not surprisingly, for wildlife. The woods shelter rabbits, raccoons, and chipmunks; old-timers swear to seeing deer.

Birds are present in great variety and abundance, particularly in winter. Barred and barn owls come to Hunter's Island in November, and long-eared owls can be seen there in the groves all winter long. Offshore are canvasback ducks, horned grebes, and other waterfowl. Twin Islands hosts great cormorants.

At the end of the boat basin a point of land juts out. The left fork of the trail cuts through the reeds to the rocky elevation at the tip of the point. The trail to the right, up the hillside, leads to the height of land where Hunter's mansion once stood. A small brook comes down the hillside here; the water is known for its sweetness, and people have long come to collect it in containers.

To view the site of Hunter's mansion, bear right up the hill, following the trail to the evergreen grove. The grove was part of the mansion garden on top of the hill; the mansion itself was set in the grove. In its day it was one of the great houses; President Martin Van Buren visited here in 1839. The house was built in Georgian style, somewhat similar to the City Hall in Manhattan. A veranda overlooked formal gardens that extended to the edge of the sound. The interior was luxurious and the walls were hung with the paintings of such old masters as Rembrandt, Rubens, Titian, and Leonardo da Vinci.

The city bought this land in 1890 and the mansion stood empty for many years. Vandalized, it was demolished in the 1930s when the Orchard Beach project was being built. Today all that remains is the pine grove that once shaded the house.

Take the road that leads back down roughly in the direction you came from. This was Hunter's road; the red sandstone bases that supported the gates can still be seen, flanking the road as it goes down to the water and the site of the now vanished bridge.

Back at the shore, you can explore out on the point or continue along the water's edge to the right. Soon a side trail splits out and toward another, smaller point. Here an enormous gray boulder juts out of the water. The boulder is a glacial erratic, a rock carried to this spot by a glacier and left behind when the glacier melted. The Siwanoy called the rock Gray Mare; it and Mishow, another erratic located near the north end of Orchard Beach, were sacred to the Indians. The rock is a good place to sit for a view of the rocky

shoreline to the north. The large building here is the New York Ath-
letic Club, with Glen Island just across the water and David's Island
farther to the northeast; the low structures on David's Island are part
of the Fort Slocum Military Reservation.

When you leave the rock and swing out to the coastline along
Long Island Sound, the shore becomes rockier than it was along the
marshy inland shore. This is the southernmost point on the east
coast of North America where the shoreline is rocky. The bedrock
has a complex geological history and dates back about half a billion
years. This is much older than the Sound itself, which was a river
valley until the postglacial rising waters flooded it.

A walk on the rocks will reveal the gradients of seashore life. In the
first zone, the zone covered only intermittently by water, barnacles
adhere to the rock. Next comes seaweed, a brown algae, along with
blue mussels and green sea lettuce. Lower down one finds red algae.
Finally, the muddy shallows between Hunter's Island and Twin Islands, the rocky finger of land to the east, form the habitat of mussels
and large clams.

Continue on to the causeway that connects Hunter's Island with
Twin Islands. Beyond the causeway, built with the rubble from the
mansion, is a large grassy area that makes a fine site for lunch. On a
sunny day the sailboats dance across the Sound, while motorboats
chug to and fro. Fishing charters out of City Island pass by, heading
out to deeper water. Every so often a large freighter comes along,
bound for the piers of New York Harbor.

Walk out to the end of Twin Islands. Here, on a rocky outcropping barely connected to the mainland, rock shelters have been constructed over the years. Benches, tables, and fireplaces add to the
comforts. The builders, mainly older people of Germanic and Slavic
backgrounds, have been coming here for many years from their
homes elsewhere in the area. Their story is told by Elizabeth Barlow
in her excellent book, *Forests and Wetlands of New York City* (Little, Brown, and Company; 1971). Also on Twin Islands are
wildflowers, including several kinds of wild mustard, asparagus, pine-
apple grass, and wild garlic.

Walk back on Twin Islands to the northern end of Orchard
Beach. Step out onto the promenade. The beach sweeps before you, a
crescent of fine sand a mile long and two hundred yards wide. On a

hot Sunday in August the crowd and din will be incredible, but on any relatively cool day when school is in session there will be few distractions from the breathtaking vista. Just offshore are Hart Island, High Island (with the radio antenna), and City Island, with its picturesque houses and boatbuilders' workshops jutting out over the water.

Almost all this beach is constructed on fill. As late as the 1920s, Hunter's Island was an island in fact as well as in name. Some swimming facilities had been developed in the park, including a garish granite boathouse and a sea wall so poorly located that except at low tide there was no beach below it at all. The facilities were not public but were for the use of various well-connected political figures, who had about three hundred bungalows built on the public land for their own use.

Then, in the 1930s, another of Robert Moses' great beaches was built here. All the old construction was taken out. Tons of garbage were dumped in the shallows between Rodman's Neck and Hunter's Island. The parking lot was paved, covering the fill; and the present bathhouses, stands, picnic areas, courts, and playgrounds were constructed. Bargeload after bargeload of fine-grained white sand was floated up from the Rockaways to the Bronx to complete the project.

Follow the esplanade. About a hundred yards beyond the end of the bathhouse are twin low brick structures next to the esplanade. Here the car owners will have to decide whether to go on and then double back later, or return to their cars now. The bus users can look for a path leading from between the two buildings, across the grass, and into the woods along the shore. The path skirts the water, running through bushes as high as an adult's head. It is a wide trail, easy to follow, and leads a few hundred yards to the mainland end of the bridge to City Island.

A scramble up the embankment puts the walker on the bridge sidewalk. City Island is a delightful New England fishing village incongruously located within the city limits of New York. Orange rowboats bob in the water just north of the bridge; they can be rented at the first house past the bridge.

Straight ahead a half block on City Island Road is the stop for the No. 12 bus back to the subway. But many walkers will want to linger awhile to explore the narrow streets and take in the nautical atmosphere of a unique New York neighborhood, visit a craft shop, and dine at one of City Island's famous seafood restaurants.

—NAT LESTER and WALT HOUCK

(As this book goes to press, the Pelham Bay Parkway Bridge is being rebuilt. The No. 12 bus has been rerouted around the construction, but it will not be possible to walk directly to Hunter's Island from the Pelham Bay subway station until completion of the project, currently expected in Winter 1984—Ed.)

WESTCHESTER COUNTY:
The Works of Man

For the walker, Westchester County is a better place to live than to visit.

The southern part of the county, roughly the part below the Cross Westchester Expressway, has ample public transportation, and the northern part has some large parks. But the whole area nearest New York City and metropolitan New Jersey has no large natural area as good for walking as Van Cortlandt Park. Worse, such areas as do exist often require that the visitor be a local resident. The areas in the northern part are hard to get to. The most attractive park in the county is Ward Pound Ridge; it is farther from the metropolitan area than is Harriman Park.

This frustrating state of affairs is partly a result of the political tension between the city and the county. By keeping parks small and restricting their usage, county officials could keep out the unwashed metrocrowd. But, in justice to Westchester politics, the main factor at work is geography.

It is geography that has shaped the works of man. Unlike Rockland and Putnam counties, with their rugged mountains and twisting valleys, Westchester is lower, with long ridges and straight valleys that lead directly to New York City. These valleys required only technology and economic demand to become high-volume transportation corridors.

Technology arrived in the 1840s; the railroads quickly and permanently shaped the land and the patterns of its use. When New York City finally reached its present boundaries, at the turn of this century, the railroads were ready to open Westchester up to new thousands. The automobile not only strengthened the already ongoing process of development but it also further inhibited the establishment of parks. In the 1890s the great incentive for the establishment of such parks as Van Cortlandt and Pelham Bay was the

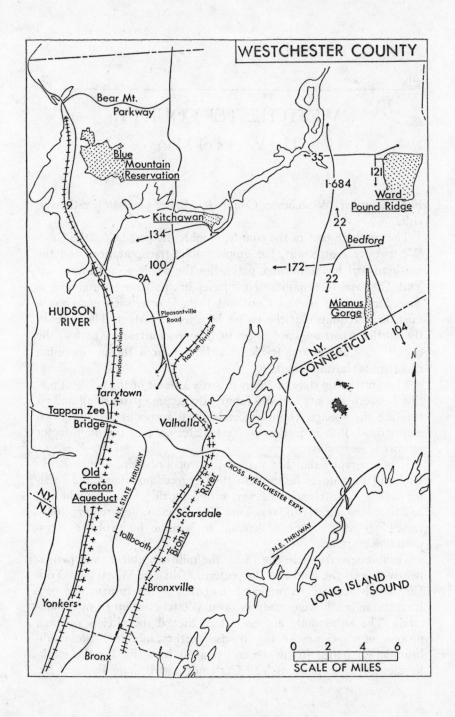

WESTCHESTER COUNTY

Bear Mt. Parkway

Blue Mountain Reservation

9

Kitchawan

134

100

9A

HUDSON RIVER

Hudson Division

Pleasantville Road

Harlem Division

Tarrytown

Tappan Zee Bridge

Valhalla

N.Y. STATE THRUWAY

Old Croton Aqueduct

Bronx River

CROSS WESTCHESTER EXPY.

Scarsdale

NY. N.J.

tollbooth

N.E. THRUWAY

Bronxville

Yonkers

Bronx

35

I-684

121

Ward Pound Ridge

22

Bedford

172

22

Mianus Gorge

N.Y. CONNECTICUT

104

N

LONG ISLAND SOUND

0   2   4   6
SCALE OF MILES

fact that large recreational preserves had to be created where the people lived. With the advent of the automobile, the citizen could hop in his flivver and head for Harriman or the distant Catskills for his walking and recreational pleasure.

As the suburbs spread out along the river valleys, golf courses took over most of the remaining natural areas of the ridges. Thus ended any lingering dream of a large park to preserve the deep woods and clear streams that Henry Hudson found.

But if the works of man have altered much in Westchester, much remains. The preserves and parks—dozens of them if all the small ones are counted—make for fine "hit-and-run" family walking: drive up, visit a favored antique or specialty shop, walk for an hour or two, drop by a farm stand, and head back home. Not for the hiking purist, perhaps, but a very workable approach to recreation.

And if the works of man have taken away, in Westchester they have given in return. The Old Croton Aqueduct and the Bronx River Parkway are both created environments, each as artificial as Riverside Park. But each offers a power of walking. As a hiker once wrote, "There are only a few places in this or any metropolitan area where a person can go out and *walk*. Just walk, not worrying about roots and rocks and climbs, but building something physical until the sweat breaks through and the muscles fall into a natural rhythm that leaves the miles behind." Here are two of these walks, each embedded in the metropolis, each an intrinsic part of its infrastructure.

The parkway walk is prettier, but the aqueduct is quieter—without the rush of traffic—and easier to follow. While much of the parkway trail is little used and almost forgotten, the aqueduct is a social experience, with joggers and bicyclists, gardeners and dog walkers, backyard mechanics and backyard cooks. The aqueduct trekkers have an additional reward, one shared with the Blue Mountain walker and other users of the railroad's Hudson Division. With good timing, these souls will find themselves on a homeward-bound train as dusk approaches, gliding sublimely along the edge of the Hudson, watching the sun set over the turrets of the Palisades. On balance, here's one vote for the works of man.

12

Bronx River North

The railroad station at Valhalla sits under quiet and brooding trees.
Even on a sunny day the spot is faintly mysterious; in an early
morning mist it becomes positively spooky. The train—an ancient
"A"-unit diesel and two creaking coaches—is gone almost before I
step onto the platform. Instinctively I huddle under the eaves of the
station as the train throbs off. As silence returns, my feet take charge.
I propel myself away from the station (which, like so many, is no
longer used as a station; this one is a restaurant) for the eleven-mile
walk down to Bronxville.

Now, eleven miles is a long walk. Many new walkers will wonder if
they can go that far. This walk will answer the question. Like the
Croton Aqueduct walk, this excursion can be of any length, because
it runs along a railroad line with stations every couple of miles. The
distance here is broken into two parts at Scarsdale, to show one way
of dividing the walk; but the walker can choose any other section
that sounds interesting.

The next train station, North White Plains, is two miles south,
with White Plains another mile and a half beyond that. This is a
good distance for those who know they need a tone-up. It also works
well for those carrying, wheeling (the path is paved), or walking with
a very young child. The Hartsdale station is another two miles south,
a good distance for the non-walker in normal condition. If at this
point all systems are still operative, just keep going.

The ride to Valhalla takes about forty-five minutes from Grand
Central Station on the Harlem Division, including a five-minute
layover in North White Plains to change trains. By car it is 15 miles
from the George Washington Bridge to Scarsdale, where you can
catch a train to Valhalla.

From the Valhalla station, cross the Bronx River Parkway at the

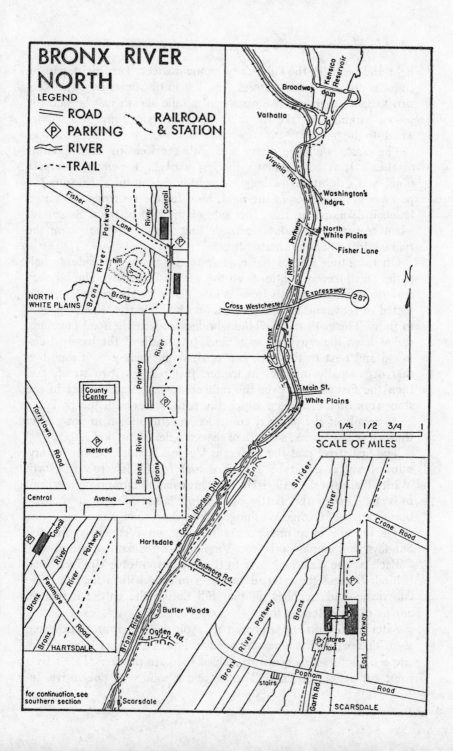

BRONX RIVER
NORTH

LEGEND

ROAD

P PARKING

RIVER

---- TRAIL

RAILROAD & STATION

Fisher Lane

Conrail

Bronx River Parkway

River

hill

Bronx

NORTH WHITE PLAINS

Bronx River Parkway

River

County Center

P metered

Tarrytown Road

Bronx River

Central   Avenue

Conrail

Bronx River Parkway

Fenimore Road

Bronx River

HARTSDALE

Broadway

Kensico Reservoir

Valhalla

Virginia Rd.

Washington's hdqrs.

North White Plains

Fisher Lane

Bronx River Parkway

Cross Westchester   Expressway   287

Bronx

Main St.

White Plains

0   1/4   1/2   3/4   1
SCALE OF MILES

Conrail (Harlem Div.)

Hartsdale

Fenimore Rd.

Butler Woods

Ogden Rd.

Strider

River

Crone Road

Bronx River Parkway

Bronx

P

stores
taxi

Bronx River

Popham

stairs

Garth Rd.

East Parkway

Road

SCARSDALE

for continuation, see
southern section

Scarsdale

N

light and head for the village's quiet main street. Turn right, passing coffee shops and grocery stores (the last until Scarsdale). The Kensico Dam Plaza is about a quarter of a mile ahead: just beyond the school parking lot, take the faint path that goes through a balsam woods to the plaza.

The plaza is a huge grassy area with the Kensico Dam looming overhead. It is large enough for flea markets, fire-engine competitions, and exhibitions of huge wrought-iron sculptures. Keeping the parkway at a distance to the right, head for the far corner, toward a baseball diamond on the other side of the line of trees. Be careful when crossing the wide side roads that come into the plaza; the traffic is infrequent but inattentive.

On the other side of the road from the plaza is a wide asphalt path. This bikeway continues all the way to Hartsdale. The bikeway is quite new; the section from White Plains to Hartsdale was completed in 1981, and further sections may be built after this book goes to press. The path has well-built bridges and, at the road crossings, scaled-down highway-type STOP signs. Just south of the baseball diamond and next to the path is a small skiing area, with a rope tow that occasionally operates in winter. Just past are two streets and then the first viaduct over the railroad tracks. A plaque set in the stonework of the viaduct, which the path shares with the parkway, gives details of the parkway construction: completion in 1925, after thirteen years of work, a length of sixteen miles, sixty footbridges.

The first street past the viaduct is Virginia Road. Here the history-minded walker can take a short detour to the left toward North White Plains to the Miller House. This colonial farmhouse was built in 1738. During the Battle of White Plains in 1776, it was the headquarters of George Washington for a short time.

The house is open from 10 A.M. to 4 P.M. on Wednesdays through Sundays, and admission is free. Virginia Road is narrow, so use care.

Back on the trail, look over to the left as you leave Virginia Road behind. Beyond the railroad yard is a hillside with a flagpole. The Americans had trenches on that hill during the battle; it was an anchor of the defensive line.

After a mile on the asphalt path, you will reach an unexpected stop. The path skirts a marshy pond and quits at Fisher Lane. Opposite is a knoll, which evidently baffled the path planners. Don't try a short cut across the knoll. The far side is solid with poison ivy. Instead, go left, toward the railroad undercrossing. Passing the parking lot, look for a sidewalk that runs along the foot of the railroad embankment. This path comes to a pedestrian tunnel under the tracks, where another path emerges and heads out in a parklike setting under high trees. (Incidentally, some people may want to start the walk here in North White Plains, to take advantage of the more frequent train service.)

The path continues through the meadow, crossing occasional suburban streets. Soon the walkway passes under the cavernous bridge for the Cross Westchester Expressway. Beyond the expressway, the trail crosses another grassy meadow, past thickets of waving purple loosestrife.

At the parking lot of the County Center, the meadow narrows. The path runs along the base of the railroad embankment and past the bus station at Main Street in White Plains. On the other side of a ramp from the parkway, cross the Bronx River on a new bridge. The path now follows a narrow right of way between the river on the left and the parkway on the right, with a hillside above the parkway. Stop for a moment to contemplate that hillside. Although from here there is very little sign of it, you are crossing an important battlefield of the American Revolution.

After the British were forced out of Boston at the beginning of the war, Howe's redcoats began a campaign to win control of the Hudson Valley and thereby split the thirteen colonies. Washington and 23,000 untried troops tried to stop the British veterans on Long Island, but British command of the sea and superior training soon broke colonial lines.

The Americans retreated rapidly up Manhattan Island, despite Washington's efforts to stop them and form a defensive line—an enduring image is that of Washington on his horse at about the present-day intersection of 42nd Street and Fifth Avenue in midtown Manhattan, shouting at his troops, pleading and threatening as they streamed by him, finally hurling his hat down in despair and shouting, "Are these the men with whom I am to defend America? Good God! Have I such troops as those?"

But American resistance did stiffen. The colonial troops turned on the redcoats at Harlem Heights, near the location of Grant's Tomb in Riverside Park. And, in today's Pelham Bay Park, Colonel Glover

and his Massachusetts soldiers bushwhacked a British column sent to
cut off the American retreat into Westchester.

The battered American force continued its retreat, marching up
the west side of the Bronx River to this point, Chatterton Hill. Here
Washington stretched a defensive line across Westchester as far as a
millpond near Silver Lake. Two guns and 1,600 men under Colonel
Alexander Hamilton waited on top of the hill. The British lined up
on the other side of the Bronx River, about where the bus station
and railroad station are now, and began a long-range artillery bom-
bardment. Other redcoats circled around to the west and advanced.
The American militia opposite them broke and fled.

With their flank exposed, the Americans withdrew, first to Miller
Hill, the slope you saw before with the flagpole, and then to North
Castle. Howe did not seek another battle. He had New York, which
was what he wanted, but the American army had survived.

It all seems remote now, and hard to pull together. But in walking
around the New York area you will encounter more and more signs
of what a struggle the war was. Riverside Park, the Bronx River, and
Pelham Bay Park are not the only areas to be touched by the war.
The Palisades . . . where Howe sent Cornwallis after the Battle of
White Plains to attack Fort Lee. While his troops clambered up the
Palisades slope, Cornwallis took his ease in a tavern that still stands
by the Shore Path.

Princeton and Kingston . . . where Washington tried to repeat his
success after he struck the sleeping Hessians at Trenton at the end of
that same year. He fought a successful skirmish at Princeton, tricked
the British at Kingston, and escaped to winter quarters at Morristown.

Suffern . . . where Washington marched in the difficult days at
the beginning of 1777. A new British army under Burgoyne was
poised at the upper end of the Hudson Valley. Washington had to
guess the British plans. Would Howe go north to join Burgoyne's advancing force? Or would he use his formidable navy to capture Philadelphia? Washington advanced to meet the greater threat, marching
up the Hudson to the Highlands at Suffern to block the British junction in the valley. Howe went to Philadelphia. Washington followed, to hardship and glory at Valley Forge.

Dobbs Ferry . . . on the Old Croton Aqueduct, where the American army in 1780 gathered to try to retake New York. The British

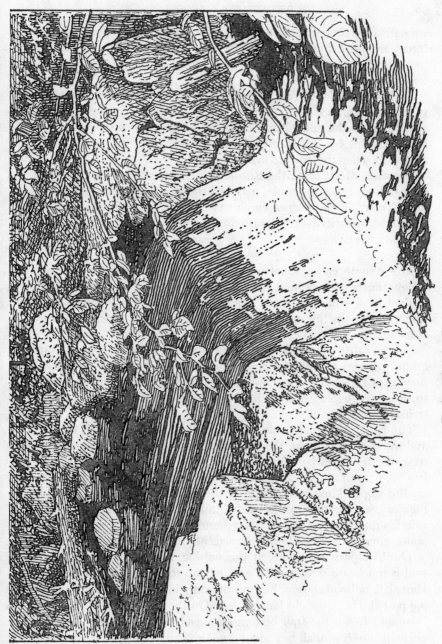

Butler Woods, Bronx River North

strengthened their forces in the city. Washington then swung his forces around behind Staten Island and suddenly made a lightning march to Virginia, trapping the exposed force at Yorktown and effectively ending the war.

And Van Cortlandt Park . . . with the southernmost American observation point east of the Hudson, at Vault Hill. The vast parade ground below the hill, where baseball and rugby now prevail, was the starting point for the triumphant American march back into New York City when the war was finally over.

For most of a decade the Revolutionary struggle continued along the Hudson. Powerful armies marched the width and breadth of this land. Today, in the rush of current events, the signs of their passage go almost unnoticed—as unnoticed as the power lines and aqueducts that sustain our lives.

At the south end of Chatterton Hill a highway viaduct crosses the valley, the river, trail, and railroad. About a hundred feet past the viaduct, a footbridge crosses the river. The path goes under the tracks, slants up the hill, and reaches the first of a series of grassy clearings. Rude stone benches are provided for the weary.

On the other side of the clearings the trail is entirely in woods, on a bluff perhaps twenty feet above the river, which is rocky and fast-flowing at this point. The railroad tracks are on the other side; every so often the quiet is stirred by a loud whoooosshh! as a passenger train roars by.

The upper trail finally comes down to the water's edge and then it and the river cross under the highway. Now, with the highway to the west, the trail rises far above the river on a steep dirt bank, with the large and comfortable houses of White Plains visible a little farther up the slope. Then, unexpectedly, the river curves back under the highway, leaving the trail to cut behind the tennis courts of the private County Tennis Club of Westchester. Next to the trail is a small pond, where fat goldfish swim complacently.

The bike path ends here, at this writing, and the next section of trail is much less developed. Cross the two roads leading over to the Hartsdale railroad station. Stay on the east side of the parkway, walking past the backyards of large houses. On the second street, which is Fenimore Road, the trail becomes a gravel path, and then it unexpectedly enters a small but wild area. This thirty-acre forest was a donation of Mrs. Emily Butler at the time the parkway was built. In this mini-forest are two streams, a ravine, numerous side trails, and many benches for sitting. This is the place to stop for lunch, five miles and about two hours from the start at Valhalla.

Regretfully the forest comes to an end, as the trail leaves the woods at the second street light north from Ogden Road on the parkway. There is no path the rest of the way to Scarsdale, a quarter of a mile ahead. Some walkers cross the road here, just where the northbound and southbound lanes separate. On the other side of the parkway is a path along the river that goes under the railroad tracks and comes out downriver from the Scarsdale station. I avoid this detour: not only is a highway crossing something to be avoided, but the river section there is polluted with trash except after a heavy rain.

At the interchange of roads at Scarsdale, the parkway makes a right turn onto a bridge across the river and tracks. Do not follow the highway but take the street toward the Scarsdale station and parking lot. Go right and into the shed along the tracks. Take the pedestrian overpass to the southbound platform. From here you can head back to Grand Central. Or you can continue the walk south by reading on to the next walk, Bronx River South.

—S. Fox

13

Bronx River South

The walk from Scarsdale to Bronxville is a jaunt for kids and their families. This four-mile section is a good length and is more continuously interesting than its neighboring section to the north; like the northern section, the pathway is level and easily followed. The central part of the walk is a path worn into grass by innumerable feet and bicycle tires. Farther south the walk follows the shore of two large and scenic ponds. One point to remember: for several summers the county on Sundays has closed a section of the parkway to autos and opened it to bicyclists. Although this complicates access, the quiet adds much to the pleasure of walking.

Train riders will take a Harlem Division train out of Grand Central to Scarsdale. Car users can arrange to use two cars, or they can leave the car near the Bronxville station and take the train to Scarsdale.

Having gotten to Scarsdale, the walker will be standing on the northbound platform with nothing in view that looks remotely like a trailway. Cross over to the southbound platform on the pedestrian bridge to get to the west side of the tracks. At the bottom of the steps is a parking lot. Cross the lot and follow its access road past a gas station to the intersection of Garth Road and Popham Road (which becomes Ardsley Road on the other side of the parkway).

Continue ahead on Garth Road, with an ice cream parlor and a grocery store on the left and a sunken glade of the park on the right. About a hundred and fifty yards south of Popham Road on Garth, a dirt road angles off behind the first stores on the right side of the street. Follow this road, which soon becomes a wide gravel path lined with park benches. Tall trees grow on both sides. Comfortable brick apartment buildings rise to the left. To the right the ground drops off into a thicket, with the Bronx River occasionally visible through the foliage.

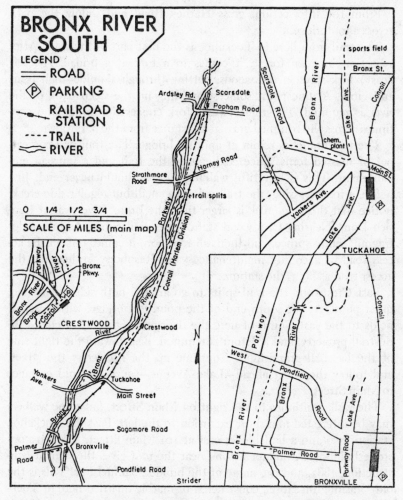

In a half mile, the path nears the parkway and gradually descends. Just before the traffic light where Harney Road crosses the parkway, the trail becomes indistinct. One branch follows the edge of the parkway; the other crosses a patch of grass to Garth Road. Follow either branch to the intersection. At the intersection, you will see behind you and to the right—between the lanes of the parkway—a pond that is the year-round home of ducks and a stop-off in spring and fall for migrating Canada geese. Benches invite resting and viewing.

From the intersection, cross Harney Road and follow the path across a footbridge.

The trail from here to Tuckahoe is the best part of the walk. After a section in open forest, it comes to a fork at a bridge. The left (east) fork stays in the woods, cutting through shoulder-high ferns and vines. At one point some scrambling up the steep bank of the river is required. The right (west) fork crosses the bridge and continues across the trimmed grass at a distance from the parkway.

The two branches rejoin at another bridge. The trail passes a carpet of massed ferns squeezed between the trail and a railroad embankment. This is beautiful walking, and it should never end. Just before a road crossing, the trail crosses a small but regular side creek; notice that this side creek is larger than the Bronx River was at Kensico Dam. Nearing Crestwood station, the trail climbs a bluff under fragrant white spruce, and then, all too soon, it comes out on the access road of a county maintenance yard. Raspberry bushes line the access road as far as the station.

Past Crestwood the trail splits to go around both sides of a large, quiet pond. At the south end of the pond is a bridge, with baseball fields to the east. South of here the river passes through a closed industrial property, and a detour is required. Bear toward the right side of the baseball grandstand. Continue up the rise, cross the street, and follow the street ahead—Lake Avenue—south past old cottages to Main Street.

The walk continues to the right on Main Street, but some walkers may be interested in a short excursion to the left. Past the Tuckahoe station, two and a half blocks east at 101 Main Street, is a two-story stone building. A builder's stone near the roof gives the year of construction, 1883, and the name of the builder, Samuel Fee. This is the old Washington Hotel, constructed of marble quarried here in Tuckahoe. The marble industry once thrived here and elsewhere in Westchester County, before improved transport opened the way to the less accessible but superior marble of Vermont. Note the rough quality of the marble in this building. The hotel was built to serve traveling businessmen in the marble trade; now it houses a woodworking shop and a sporting-apparel outlet on the ground floor.

Returning to Lake Avenue and Main Street, continue west on Main Street to the bridge over the Bronx River, which is a chan-

Bronx River at Bronxville

nelized ditch through the U.S.V. Pharmaceutical Corporation's industrial complex.

The bridge over the river is a spot on which to appreciate the history of the Bronx River Parkway. At the turn of the century a local resident, William Niles, returned from Scotland impressed with the beauty of the Ness River as it passed through the city of Inverness. Over the next ten years his tireless promotion of a linear park along the Bronx River gradually won support.

Land was purchased by the county of Westchester and the city of New York. Over three hundred and fifty structures were removed along the route. Only this complex remains. At its heart stands one of the earliest cotton mills in this country. The mill is currently the engineering shop of the complex; it is the two-story stone structure barely visible over the roof of the first building on the left side of the river. (For a better view of the old mill, walk past the complex and look back; it is the second building in from the street.)

Continue west along Main Street to the rise ahead. Where Main turns sharply right, make a sharp left turn and continue down the hillside to the river, flowing again in natural banks. Cross the river on the bridge of a little-used access road behind the Parkway Casino.

From here south to Garrett Street, there's no specific trail, just a stroll through a tree-shaded meadow. On the other side of Garrett Street, the greenbelt widens for another large pond. The pond is shallow and silted. Ducks seem to stand on the water. In the deeper sections, goldfish can be seen. Where the trail splits, stay on the left (east) side of the pond; this puts maximum distance between hiker and highway.

The glade at the south end of the pond is a tight fit between the parkway on one side and an apartment house just across the rocky gorge of the river; it nevertheless is one of the picturesque vistas of Westchester County for its view of trees and footbridge, with the pond beyond reflecting the foliage.

The path crosses West Pondfield Road and follows a newly paved path to Palmer Road, the end of this walk. The trail continues only a little farther. At this writing the recently rebuilt interchange of the parkway with the Cross County Parkway does not include any provision whatever for the footpath. Groups are working to link the Westchester walk to the unmaintained but still passable section in the Bronx, so that in the future this walk may be extended all the way to the hemlock forest in the New York Botanical Garden in Bronx Park.

At Palmer Road turn left (east) to the nearby Bronxville station, passing a Chinese restaurant and a pastry shop. Trains come every hour. Tickets to Grand Central are inexpensive, and the trip takes only about half an hour—enough time to let the feet cool and to start a few thoughts about hot showers and cold drinks.

—S. Fox

Old Croton Aqueduct

For well over a century the Old Croton Aqueduct pathway has been a favorite trail for year-round easy walking. The pathway traverses pristine woodlands and meadowlands, estates, abandoned farms, and suburban as well as urban areas. There are splendid views of the Hudson River and the Palisades, which the path parallels for much of its route. The excursion described here runs about eleven miles from Tarrytown to Yonkers, but this walk can easily be shortened or lengthened to suit the inclination of the walker.

Unlike today's superhighways and industrial complexes, which often obliterate whatever stands in their way, the great engineering projects of the mid-nineteenth century—the railroads, canals, and aqueducts—left their natural surroundings largely intact. The area traversed by the Old Croton Aqueduct has retained much of the bucolic atmosphere that prevailed before its construction. Dogwood, mountain laurel, and other shrubs are in full bloom along the trail in the spring, and in the summer blackberries abound. The wooded portions include hemlock, pine, oak, birch, Norway maple, black cherry, mulberry, and sassafras. Among the birds observed in the vicinity of the aqueduct are cardinals, red-winged blackbirds, robins, bluejays, crows, pheasants, and migrating Canada geese. The alert walker may spot rabbits, woodchucks, deer, raccoons, and even an occasional badger.

The geology of the area traversed by the trail was described by the aqueduct's chief engineer, John B. Jervis:

> The soil, earth and rock of the country from the banks of the Croton to the City of New York is of one general character. The line cuts a small section of marble of inferior quality . . . it passes . . . marble of pretty fair quality for building . . . at Dobbs Ferry and Hastings. . . . With these limited exceptions, the prevailing rock . . . is gneiss, of great variety in quality. . . . The surface soil

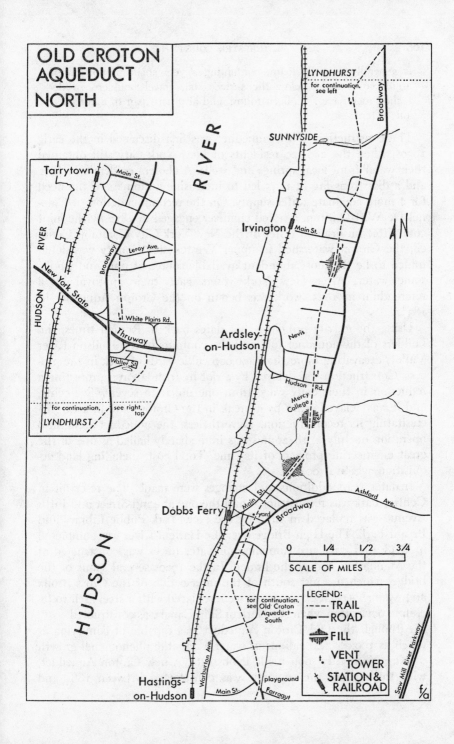

OLD CROTON AQUEDUCT
NORTH

RIVER

Tarrytown

Main St.

RIVER

Broadway

Leroy Ave.

HUDSON

New York State

Thruway

White Plains Rd.

Walter St.

for continuation, see right, top

LYNDHURST

LYNDHURST

for continuation, see left

Broadway

SUNNYSIDE

Irvington   Main St.

N

Ardsley-on-Hudson

Nevis

Hudson Rd.

Mercy College

Ashford Ave.

Dobbs Ferry   Main St.   Broadway

yard

0   1/4   1/2   3/4

SCALE OF MILES

HUDSON

for continuation, see Old Croton Aqueduct–South

LEGEND:

- - - - TRAIL

━━━━ ROAD

FILL

VENT TOWER

STATION & RAILROAD

Warburton Ave.

Saw Mill River Parkway

Hastings-on-Hudson   Main St.   Farragut   playground

f/a

is generally a sandy loam, containing a very small proportion of argillaceous earth. Below the surface soil, gravel boulders, or detached rock have . . . been found, and also hard pan to a considerable extent.

The construction of the aqueduct was first discussed in the early 1830s, when the 280,000 residents of New York City still obtained their water from local springs and wells. A cholera epidemic in 1832 and a disastrous fire in 1835 led to increasing awareness of the need for a more adequate water supply. On the recommendation of Colonel De Witt Clinton, a noted engineer engaged in 1832 by the joint committee on fire and water of the New York City Common Council, the Croton watershed in upper Westchester County was determined to be the most abundant available source of pure and wholesome water. After New York voters gave their approval by a referendum in 1835, work was begun on the Croton Aqueduct in 1837.

Using the gravity principle that dates back to Roman times, the builders of the aqueduct followed the contours of the Hudson River Valley, excavating more than 400,000 cubic yards of rock in the process. Construction was delayed by a riot by Irish laborers protesting a reduction in their daily wage from one dollar to seventy-five cents, and it was delayed again by a break in the Croton dam in 1840, necessitating its reconstruction. Nevertheless, the aqueduct went into operation on July 4, 1842, and was immediately hailed as one of the great engineering projects of its time. Total cost, including land acquisition, was $12,500,000.

In later years additions and changes were made. The reservoir in Central Park was reconstructed and the one at 42nd Street and Fifth Avenue was replaced in time by the New York Public Library and Bryant Park. The High Bridge over the Harlem River was completed in 1848; in 1872 a neo-Romanesque water tower was constructed at the Manhattan end of the bridge. In the 1920s several spans of the bridge, which lies just south of the intersection of the Cross Bronx and Major Deegan expressways, were replaced with a steel arch to facilitate navigation when the Harlem Ship Canal was constructed.

Although the Old Croton Aqueduct was capable of conveying as much as 100,000,000 gallons of water a day, the phenomenal growth of New York City soon made it obsolete. A new Croton Aqueduct, with three times the capacity, was constructed between 1884 and

1893; no trail was included in that project. When this water source also proved inadequate, it was supplemented by the Catskill Aqueduct system, built between 1907 and 1917, which more than doubled the city's water supply. A trail on top of this aqueduct may be followed, with many interruptions, from Yonkers all the way to the Catskill region.

Leaky and expensive to maintain, the Old Croton Aqueduct was taken out of service to New York City in 1955, although its service to some suburban communities existed until 1965. It soon fell into neglect. Towns found its right of way ideal for parking lots and schoolyards, and residents incorporated handy segments into their backyards. Rather than fight, New York City's Department of Water and Gas, which controlled the right of way, often issued permits allowing such uses. Finally, in 1966, at the urging of the Croton Aqueduct Association, the New York/New Jersey Trail Conference, and other outdoor groups, the state under Governor Nelson Rockefeller assumed responsibility for the trail north of the New York City line. Strategic spots of the trail have been blazed with yellow disks, and new park facilities have been developed along some sections of the path.

Those portions of the aqueduct that have been lost may never be recovered, but most of the trail has been preserved or restored for hikers, joggers, cyclists, equestrians, and local residents. Starting at the Croton dam a little south of Peekskill, the aqueduct travels thirty-two miles to its terminal point at 173rd Street in upper Manhattan. Elevation at the dam is 166 feet above mean tide; from here the aqueduct descends 46.3 feet at the rate of 13.25 inches per mile, maintaining this declivity across hills and valleys by means of excavations and embankments. The trail runs along a right of way averaging sixty-six feet in width. Underground, beneath the trail, is an oval tube of laid-up stone with interior dimensions of about eight by nine feet.

The longest continuous stretch of the aqueduct runs about nine miles from a point slightly south of the Tappan Zee Bridge down to Yonkers, about 10 miles north of the George Washington Bridge. Access to the beginning is either from Tarrytown or Irvington, depending on how far the walker wants to go. Since the path runs parallel to the railroad and a few blocks east of it, hikers may walk whatever distance they wish. The railroad has stops every few miles and runs about once an hour; the Conrail schedule for the Hudson Division will give details and indicate local stops.

Those starting the walk from Tarrytown should head east toward the hill from the station. After circling the station plaza, follow Main Street uphill to Broadway and head south. A little before the Tappan Zee Bridge, a portion of the aqueduct has been preserved east of Broadway. This section runs from Leroy Avenue to the Cross Westchester Expressway. Turn left onto Leroy and walk a few paces. Soon the street bears left. To the right at this point is the parking lot of a clinic; the aqueduct is the embankment running along the right (west) edge of the parking lot.

Another short stretch extends for about a quarter of a mile from just south of the bridge. From Broadway, head east on Walter Street for a short distance, then follow the road that goes diagonally to the left. After a while there is a wide, bushy right of way, which is the aqueduct. Continue southward along the path until it ends at a private drive, then head back west to Broadway.

A short distance south, about half a mile from the Tappan Zee approach and two hundred yards south of the traffic light where the private drive meets Broadway, the aqueduct path goes through an opening in the stone wall on the west side of Broadway and cuts diagonally through the Lyndhurst estate. The well-manicured nineteenth-century country estate of the railroad tycoon Jay Gould, this property now belongs to the National Trust for Historic Preservation, which allows the grounds to be used for occasional art auctions, flea markets, dog shows, summer music festivals, and other events. The main building, a Gothic Revival villa, is open to visitors for a fee.

From Lyndhurst, the aqueduct is easily followed all the way to Yonkers. Every mile or so the right of way is marked with the chimney-like white stone towers that once served as ventilators and pressure equalizers. Less frequently, large square structures are encountered; these contained weirs that cleaned any floating debris from the water in the aqueduct.

Proceeding down the Hudson, the trail crosses Sunnyside Lane. Down the hill to the right is Sunnyside, the home of nineteenth-century author Washington Irving. This charming cottage, described by its creator as being "as full of angles and corners as a cocked hat," is an engrossing assemblage of gables, a tower, and weather vanes, with

Old Croton Aqueduct, Irvington, New York

gardens all around. The house and gardens are open to the public for a fee.

A little farther on is the town of Irvington. Walkers who want to avoid the long stretch of pavement out of Tarrytown may start the walk here, hiking up Main Street from the railroad station to where the aqueduct crosses at Irvington High School. A short distance south is an excellent view of the Hudson and the surrounding area; here the aqueduct runs high above a valley on an embankment, with a city street tunneling far beneath it.

South of Irvington the trail passes a spectacular if somewhat run-down house on the right. The Armour-Stiner house is an ornate oc-tagonal structure topped by an enormous dome. The house was origi-nally built in 1860 and remodeled in 1872 after the then popular French Second Empire style. Its octagonal shape reflects the theories of a contemporary thinker, Orson Squire Fowler, who wrote, "The Octagonal form is . . . beautiful as well as capacious, and more con-sonant with the predominant or governing form of Nature."

Soon after, near Ardsley, a stately columned mansion stands to the right of the aqueduct. This is Nevis, built by Alexander Hamilton's son in 1835. It now houses the offices of a branch of Columbia Uni-versity that conducts experiments in nuclear physics.

The aqueduct crosses the campus of Mercy College, a Catholic women's liberal arts institute. Just beyond is Dobbs Ferry, named

Old Croton Aqueduct near Dobbs Ferry, after photo by Henry Sloan

after Jeremiah Dobbs, who operated a ferry across the neutral waters
of the Hudson during the American Revolution. According to some
historians, it was in Dobbs Ferry that General Washington and the
French commander Rochambeau met in 1781 to plan the Yorktown
campaign that ended the Revolution; the house in which these historic meetings were said to have taken place burned down a few
years ago.

Just before the trail crosses to the east side of Broadway, it passes
through a maintenance yard for state equipment; this was the home
and maintenance center for the supervisor of this section of the
aqueduct. The train station in Dobbs Ferry can be reached by turning right on any of the small streets before the Broadway crossing
and then turning left on Main Street.

In Hastings-on-Hudson the trail passes a large park, a good spot
for lunch break. Just after the park, the trail crosses a major road intersection. The Hastings train station is down Main Street from the
point where the aqueduct recrosses Broadway; at Warburton Ave-

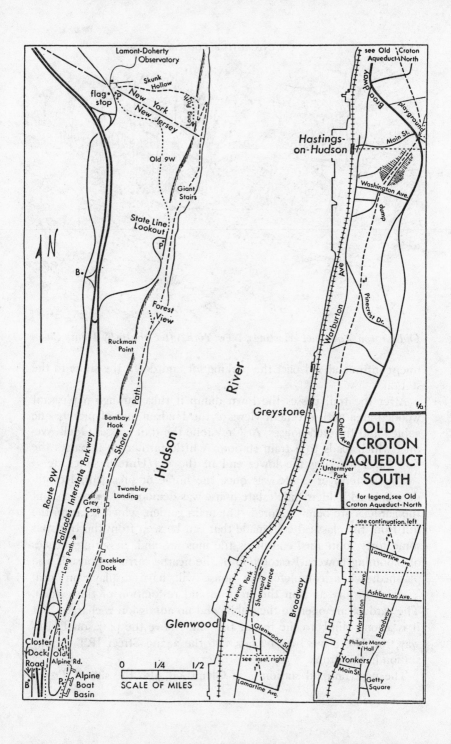

Lamont-Doherty Observatory

Skunk Hollow

flag stop

New York
New Jersey

Long Path

Old 9W

Giant Stairs

State Line Lookout

P

B.

Forest View

Ruckman Point

Shore Path

Bombay Hook

Hudson

River

Grey Crag

Twombley Landing

Excelsior Dock

Route 9W

Palisades Interstate Parkway

Long Path.

Closter Dock Road

Old Alpine Rd.

B

P.

Alpine Boat Basin

N

see Old Croton Aqueduct-North

Broadway

playground

Hastings-on-Hudson

Main St.

Washington Ave.

dump

Warburton Ave.

Pinecrest Dr.

Greystone

Odell Ave.

Untermyer Park

OLD CROTON AQUEDUCT — SOUTH

for legend, see Old Croton Aqueduct - North

see continuation, left

Lamartine Ave.

Ashburton Ave.

Warburton Ave.

Broadway

Philipse Manor Hall

Yonkers

Main St.

Getty Square

Trevor Park

Shonnard Terrace

Broadway

Glenwood St.

Glenwood

see inset, right

Lamartine Ave.

0   1/4   1/2
SCALE OF MILES

Old Croton Aqueduct, Hastings, New York, after photo by Henry Sloan

nue, continue ahead past the parking lot and down the stairs to the station.

After the trail passes the town dump it runs through a pleasant wooded area with excellent views of the Hudson and of picturesque gabled and turreted houses. At Greystone the trail crosses Odell Avenue, which leads to a train station. A little farther on it passes the lion gates marking the lower end of the old Untermyer estate.

The Untermyer estate was once the home of presidential candidate Samuel Tilden. The estate house was demolished years ago, but the gardens are being restored. The main garden, which is far up the hill from the classical colonnade that can be seen from the trail, has some forty fountains, enormous tile mosaics, and, in spring, masses of blooming flowers. Restoration of the nearby carriage house is also planned; when complete, the house will have displays on local Yonkers history and on the creation and restoration of the garden. The gardens are open to the public and no admission is charged, but it is a long climb to the top of the hill. Above the park, on Broadway, the No. 2 bus may be taken to the 242nd Street IRT subway station in the Bronx.

The next railroad station is in Glenwood, also the site of Trevor

Park and the Hudson River Museum. The museum offers exhibits on contemporary art, science, history, and Indian culture of the Hudson Valley and includes a planetarium, library, and museum shop.

Those going beyond Glenwood will encounter increasingly urban surroundings, until the aqueduct trail comes to a halt at Lamartine Avenue in Yonkers. From here the walker can choose to return by bus or train to New York City. The No. 1 bus runs along Warburton Avenue, west of the aqueduct, and terminates at the 242nd Street subway station at Van Cortlandt Park. A walk south along Broadway through a deteriorating neighborhood will bring the walker to Getty Square, where there is more frequent bus service. The Yonkers railroad station is in the same direction: head south from Lamartine on Warburton Avenue and then west on Main Street to the station.

For walkers to Getty Square or the railroad station, there is one more point of interest on the way: Philipse Manor Hall on Warburton Avenue, a little north of Main Street. Frederick Philipse (1626–1702) was a Dutch settler said to have been Peter Stuyvesant's "architect-builder." Under British rule he became a wealthy landowner, eventually controlling lands from the Croton River to Spuyten Duyvil. His descendants, who remained loyal to the British, were forced to relinquish their lands during the Revolutionary War. His manor hall, which is currently open from 9 A.M. to 5 P.M. on Wednesdays through Sundays (free admission), is now a museum, featuring the Cochran collection of portraits of famous Americans.

The portion of the aqueduct from Irvington to Yonkers is the single longest stretch for walking, but other portions of the aqueduct still survive, and some provide excellent walking. A northern section of the trail runs for about five miles from Croton Reservoir to Ossining. The northern terminus at Croton Dam is some distance from the railroad station at Croton–Harmon, but the walk to the trailhead leads along pleasant, tree-lined suburban streets, and the stretch of trail near the dam is outstanding: a hemlock-shaded stretch that presents a tranquil, timeless atmosphere. In Ossining the path leads across a massive and spectacular bridge spanning Sing Sing Kill.

A readily accessible aqueduct walk for New York City residents, most of it through relatively unspoiled woodlands, runs from Van Cortlandt Park in the Bronx through Tibbetts Brook Park in Yonkers, covering a distance of about three and a half miles. The path extends from just west of the Major Deegan–Mosholu Parkway crossing, runs east of the Van Cortlandt Park golf course and high on the hillside on the east side of Tibbetts Brook Park, ending at the gatehouse at Yonkers Avenue where it intersects the Cross County Parkway.

Other remnants also remain, including a stretch in the Bronx and one in Manhattan. A thousand-foot section of the tunnel running through Central Park is still in use, as a storage room for the nearby Metropolitan Museum of Art.

One segment in a run-down section of Yonkers extends east from Palisades Avenue just south of Ashburton, coming out on Yonkers Avenue a little before Prescott Street. A somewhat disjointed section extends for about six and a half miles from Ossining to Tarrytown by way of the Sleepy Hollow area immortalized by Washington Irving. It includes some stretches of pleasant woodland walking as well as an equestrian path, but because of obstacles and detours it is rather difficult for the inexperienced walker to follow.

Some or all of these segments can be combined to make a long walk. One popular such trek takes the aqueduct all the way from the subway at Van Cortlandt up through Yonkers to Tarrytown. For several years this writer has led an "open-ended" Sierra Club hike along the aqueduct in September, starting either at Croton–Harmon or at Van Cortlandt Park and going for as long as people want to hike. On a few memorable occasions the intrepid trekkers have put up with the necessary street walking and detours, and have covered the entire distance in a single day.

—HENRY S. SLOAN

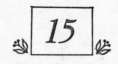

Mianus River Gorge

Scarcely 35 miles northeast of the George Washington Bridge, the Mianus River Gorge Wildlife Refuge and Botanical Preserve is a peaceful, friendly, enticing retreat: rich in historical background, geological formations, mineral deposits, and flora and fauna. It is a naturalist's preserve and a hiker's joy.

It is still being expanded; currently at 375 acres, it includes a stretch of river, the steep-sided gorge cut by the river, a 20-acre stand of virgin hemlocks up to three hundred years old, an excellent three-mile trail system discreetly marked, several outstanding views, a waterfall cascading over variegated rock formations, and an intriguing patchwork pattern of old fieldstone fences that summon reveries of a bygone farming era.

At Mianus River Gorge, requests for information or for group visits are answered courteously and promptly. In season a volunteer warden is on hand to answer questions. The pamphlet and trail map available without charge at the trail shelter at the entrance states, "We hope that you enjoy your visit and come again." There is no admission charge, but donations are always welcome at the gorge, which is privately and voluntarily supported.

The friendliness at the preserve suggests the presence of local guidance and support. The Mianus Gorge Conservation Committee was founded in 1953 to ensure "the preservation of the virgin forest and abundant wildlife along the Mianus River in Bedford, North Castle, and Pound Ridge, New York." In 1970 the gorge was registered as a Natural History Landmark by the U. S. Department of the Interior, a testimonial to the committee's success in meeting its objective. The gorge was also the very first preserve affiliated with the Nature Conservancy, the highly effective land-conservation organization.

The gorge is friendly in another important respect: it is almost im-

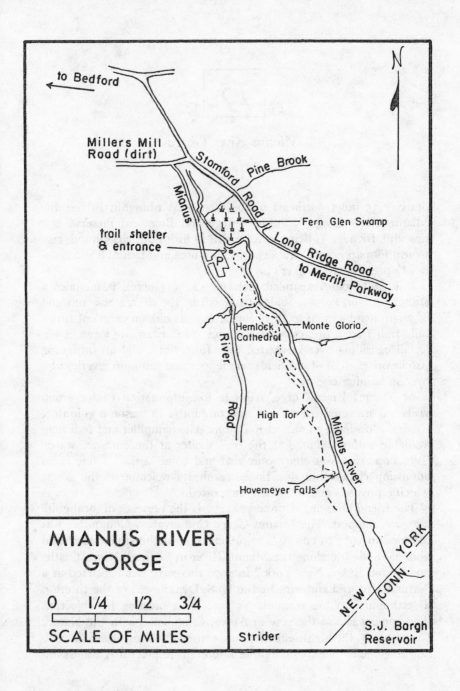

to Bedford

Millers Mill
Road (dirt)

Stamford   Pine Brook
Road

Mianus

Fern Glen Swamp

trail shelter
& entrance

Long Ridge Road
to Merritt Parkway

P

Hemlock   Monte Gloria
Cathedral

River

Road

High Tor

Mianus River

Havemeyer Falls

NEW   YORK

MIANUS RIVER
GORGE

0   1/4   1/2   3/4

SCALE OF MILES

Strider

CONN.

S.J. Bargh
Reservoir

N

possible to lose your way or fail to return to the starting point. You are bound between the river below and the road above. Only a genius of misdirection could stray from the well-trodden paths.

You can walk as much or as little as you want to. The maximum round trip is about five miles, so if your pace is leisurely, with rest stops, sights to see, and nature to absorb, allow about three and a half hours for the traverse and return.

The gorge is a preserve for all seasons, with a limitation: it is officially open only between April 1 and November 30. Plan your visiting time accordingly. The gorge is replete and resplendent with spring flowering, fall coloring, and shady summer warmth.

Even when the preserve is officially closed, the parking lot is left open on most nice days. If the lot is closed, you may park along the road and walk into the preserve.

The gorge committee has provided certain amenities at the entrance to the trail system. First, stop at the trail shelter and, if necessary, at the rest rooms (closed off season). To nature purists, these may be distressing signs of sybaritic living, but the shelter does blend in nicely with its surroundings, and the toilets are modestly set back in a wooded area away from the trail.

The entrance area is the place to eat, either in your car or on the grassy rim surrounding the parking lot, as picnicking in the preserve is not allowed in the interests of cleanliness. Also, dogs are not permitted in the preserve.

At the trail shelter pick up the brochure and trail map describing the gorge and showing you what to see and where to go to see it. A more comprehensive guide can be purchased for a modest sum from the warden at the trail shelter. Entitled "Flora and Fauna of the Mianus River Gorge," it describes the gorge in its historical, geological, and mineralogical aspects and includes a comprehensive list of the flora and fauna identified in the preserve.

Studying the individual trail map or the large-scale map at the trail shelter, you will note the various markings and the recommended returning points for those who cannot or do not wish to do it all. Sturdy shoes or sneakers are advisable.

The trails are generally smooth and well maintained. The main trail is marked with yellow arrows and red disks. There are hills, roots, and rocks, but no exhausting obstacles. The hemlock forest is a glory of peace and solitude. The tread is soft; the gurgling of the river below, the seductive music it provides, emphasizes the stillness of the hemlock cathedral.

In contrast, Havemeyer Falls, almost at the end of the trail, rushes down the precipitous hillside, cascading noisily over multifaceted and mossy rock foundations. The path from here down to the river and reservoir edge is short but steep. Step carefully and avoid embedded stones and roots; pay heed to wet, slippery leaves and roots.

Another impressive sight is at the end of a spur trail. High Tor, a high, flat rock outcropping, is a photogenic spot with a clear view over the S. J. Bargh Reservoir of the Greenwich Water Company, the depository of the Mianus River waters. The tor is about a mile and a half out from the shelter, or a total walk of about three miles.

The remains of a mica mine lie at the end of another spur trail. Mica is a brilliantly shiny mineral once popular as insulation for high-grade radio components. Through the years the flat pieces of loose mica have gradually wandered away; half the shimmering material is now gone. Please do not accelerate its disappearance.

Public transportation to the preserve is not available, but it is an easy and scenic trip by car. From the metropolitan area, take the Hutchinson River Parkway north and into the Merritt Parkway. Get off at Exit 34, Long Ridge Road, and go left toward Bedford. Continue on this road for 7.7 miles to Millers Mill Road. Turn sharp left and go 0.1 mile over the bridge to Mianus River Road, a dirt road on the left. Make a left turn and go 0.7 miles to the gorge parking entrance on the left.

For an alternative route, take Interstate 684 from where it leaves the Hutchinson River Parkway near White Plains. Get off at Route 172 (Exit 4) and take a right to picturesque Bedford Village. Turn left at the traffic light going north on Route 22; take the right fork at a grassy triangle onto Poundridge Road just before the business district of the village. Soon after, turn right at the gas station onto Stamford (Long Ridge) Road. Turn right again at the first right, Millers Mill Road, making the left turn just past the bridge and proceeding on the dirt road to the gorge parking lot.

The Mianus River Gorge Wildlife Refuge and Botanical Preserve is inviting. It has charm and atmosphere. It is a major repository of a variety of flora, fauna, habitats, geology, and history. It is photogenic and scenic. It is relaxing, peaceful, and stimulating. It is well worth a visit and well worth support.

—ARNOLD BUCHSBAUM

Ward Pound Ridge Reservation

The Indians called it Peppenegheck—"Cross River." Along its shores stood stone weirs, stretched with nets of woven dogbane fiber and deer sinew. Algonquins of the Mohegan nation and members of the Tankiteke tribe traveled its slow waters in birchbark canoes. At night they slept in bark and reed shelters, cushioned on mats of evergreen needles. The land was rich in deer and other game; the sky above was clear.

Today, the fields through which the Cross River meanders are within the boundaries of Ward Pound Ridge Reservation, a 4,365-acre preserve in Westchester County, 40 miles northeast of the George Washington Bridge. The reservation's rolling hills look out on grassy meadowlands, with tree-lined slopes and lakes beyond. Over thirty-five miles of marked trails thread through the park, including the walk described here of two and a half miles on the River Trail. Comfort stations and parking facilities are conveniently located at several sites. Ward Pound Ridge is open on weekends year round, and daily during the summer months. Nature lovers and photographers should be sure to bring along field guides and cameras.

Although not accessible by mass transit, the reservation is easily reached by car from the White Plains side of Westchester County by going north on the Saw Mill River Parkway or Route 684 to Katonah. At the junction with Route 35, turn right and proceed to the Cross River sign at the junction with Route 121. Another right, this time onto Route 121, soon brings you to the park entrance on the left. The nominal entrance fee per car is a small price to pay for a delightful day outdoors. Be sure to ask for the map of the park when you pay.

Our trail, the River Trail, follows the Cross River through the reservation from Meyer Arboretum to the Kimberly Bridge picnic area.

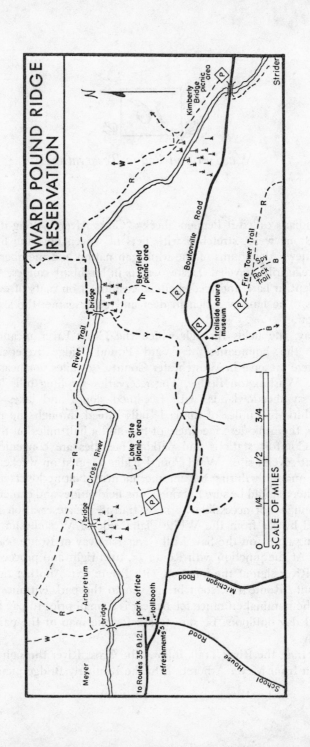

Even beginners will enjoy this trail, which invites a leisurely ramble of about an hour along a level, well-marked path.

The River Trail can be approached from four locations in the reservation—Meyer Arboretum, the Lake Site parking field, Bergfield picnic area, and Kimberly Bridge. We begin at the Lake Site parking field. Drive 0.4 mile on Boutonville Road beyond the park's toll booth and turn left. This is a good rest stop before and after the hike —there are picnic tables, rest rooms, stone fireplaces for cooking, and a parking area.

Access to the River Trail is by way of a path leading from the northeast end of the Lake Site parking field. Look for a trail leading from the water fountain at the upper left-hand corner of the field.

On a spring day the open field is dotted with blue flag and hawk-weed, daisies and forget-me-nots. The air is alive with butterflies, grasshoppers, and birds. The trail enters a shrub area, which can be swampy in spring and even in summer. It's best to wear closed shoes, since walking is easier through the muddy areas than through the dense shrubbery. You're sure to notice skunk cabbage and other wetland plants, and, if you're quiet and lucky, a chorus of frogs will greet you.

At the first bridge across the Cross River, stop awhile and, as the shallow waters ripple and babble over smoothed stones, reflect on how it was when the Indians fished here. Continue on, and you will enter an evergreen forest. It is suddenly quieter. The canopy of tall trees cushions sound, the air is crisp with the scent of pine, and the ground is soft and springy underfoot.

A snowmobile sign marks your arrival at the River Trail. To the left, the trail leads to the Meyer Arboretum, a 175-acre habitat of native trees and shrubs you may want to visit at the end of your hike. We will go to the right. The path will always have the river on our right, with circular red blazes on trees and boulders.

From time to time you will notice the remains of low stone walls alongside the trail. Erected by farmers, the walls once served to divide croplands and define property lines. In the eighteenth and nineteenth centuries this area was heavily farmed, until westward migration led to an eventual decline in population.

We return to a deciduous forest of oaks, hickory, maple, and beech. Squirrels and chipmunks scamper across the path. The trail is now grassy underfoot. Another wet area intersects our path and a conduit pipe crosses it. The river follows alongside, sometimes nearby and sometimes a small distance away.

Just before another bridge crossing, the River Trail veers to the left. Do not cross the bridge. (Remember, the river always stays to the right.) Across the bridge, another path will lead to the Bergfield picnic area in case you wish to end your walk here. A shelter (No. 7) can be found at this picnic site.

Gradually ascending and descending as it follows the contours of the hillside, the trail continues along the river's shore. Sunlight filters through the leafy canopy, capturing reflections in the still waters below. You may want to take your shoes off and refresh your feet in the cool, inviting waters.

At the top of a slope, the trail divides again. The path on the extreme right leads to the Kimberly Bridge picnic area, our final destination. It's a short walk to the picnic grounds where you can rest again before returning to your car.

Since the trail is not circular, there are several ways back to the starting point. One way is to double back along the same trail. Another, assuming you received a reservation map when you paid the entrance fee, is to fashion a return on the trails to the north of the River Trail, through Deer Hollow and out by the Arboretum. Or you can take the short cut, along the Boutonville Road, and visit the Trailside Nature Museum along the way.

Boutonville Road leaves the picnic area at the right of the bridge, goes past the Bergfield picnic area and the Trailside Museum, and continues past the Lake Site parking field. The Trailside Museum, built by the Civilian Conservation Corps, features regularly changed exhibits on various aspects of Westchester's history and the reservation itself. The relief map of the park in the museum is useful for planning other walks. The museum is also the home of the Delaware Indian Resource Center, a library dealing with North American Indian culture.

Educational programs are offered by the museum staff. You can go on an owl prowl, learn about colonial customs, or pick up pointers on flycasting. The museum is open Wednesday to Sunday from 9 A.M. to 5 P.M., and a schedule of events is available from the reservation. For a schedule, information, or maps, write the Ward Pound Ridge Reservation, Cross River, NY 10518, or call (914) 763-3493.

At this writing, plans are under way to exhibit the bones of a prehistoric mastodon at the museum. The fossilized remains were discovered by a science student in the Pound Ridge area. This is the first local evidence of these animals, which have been extinct for nine thousand years. Since fluted spear tips had previously been discovered nearby, archaeologists had hoped to establish a link between the two. Scholars from Norwalk Community College excavated the site and discovered additional animal fossils, but no direct link with ancient Indian cultures could be established.

The Trailside Museum is not the only focus of activities in the park. The reservation also has facilities for skiing, horseback riding, sleighing, and snowmobiling, although restrictions apply in some cases. Overnight permits for the twenty-four shelters in the park can be obtained at the superintendent's office. The stone and timber shelters, each with a sleeping capacity of eight, are equipped with fireplaces and picnic tables. No tent camping or trailer camping is permitted in the reservation.

The reservation is a major center of cross-country skiing. The touring trails fan out to the south from the ski touring center at shelters No. 4 and No. 5, accessible from Michigan Road within the park. In season, programs of instruction are offered; for further information, see the winter schedule of activities. Equipment can be rented in the park at a station just past the entrance toll booth.

Of course, there are always other sections of those thirty-five miles of trails to explore. On the hill west of Honey Hollow is a cave of the Leather Man, a legendary wandering hermit of the mid-nineteenth century.

The story of the Leather Man is one of the most colorful and romantic in local lore. Roaming the country roads of Westchester County and Connecticut for over thirty years, he slept in caves and dressed in a suit fashioned of leather. He rarely spoke on his regular rounds, but farmers willingly fed him and offered him lodging. A legend grew up around him, which turned out to be close to the truth when journalists and researchers gradually uncovered the facts. The Leather Man as a youth in France had loved a girl employed in his father's leather factory near Marseille. His father opposed the match, and the girl disappeared. Convinced of foul play, the youth left home, never to return.

South of the Pell Hill picnic area are the Fire Tower Trail and Spy Rock Trail. The Fire Tower Trail is a broad road leading to the highest point in the reservation. On a clear day Manhattan can be seen from this point, almost a thousand feet above sea level. The trail is fragrantly fringed with clusters of mountain laurel in spring. Spy Rock Shelter, south and west of the tower, was used by Colonel Sheldon's Light Dragoons during the Revolutionary War to observe the movements of British troops.

Other trails offer the opportunity to study the reservation's rich Indian lore. The area was under Indian control until 1640, only a hundred and thirty-five years before the Revolutionary War. A reminder of the Indian times are the Bare Rock petroglyphs, ancient Indian rock drawings in the southwest part of the park on the Dancing Rock Trail. Another reminder of the Indian past is in the name of the reservation itself. (Not the "Ward" part; this comes from William "Boss" Ward, a Westchester political power for forty years, who fought for the establishment of the park.) At the park's southern boundary, near a ridge by Raven Rocks, is a natural trap. The Indians constructed an enclosure, or pound, here. Parties of hunters, whooping and crying, would drive their prey from the surrounding areas into the pound, while other hunters kept the animals from escaping.

This is the recreational sampler—nature, culture, geology, and history—that Ward Pound Ridge's lush woods and rolling hillsides provide the solitary walker, families, and groups. Pack your enthusiasm along with a picnic lunch and come prepared for a fresh and invigorating day in the outdoors.

—STEPHANIE FOGEL

17

Kitchawan Research Station

Kitchawan Research Station is a park of much diversity, with a wide range of activities, a variety of forest types, and many sites of historical interest. Nearly every kind of northeastern tree and every stage of forest succession is represented in the park, located on the south side of the Croton Reservoir in Westchester County, 30 miles northeast of the George Washington Bridge. The five miles of hiking trails pass through such forest types as hemlock, maple-beech-hickory, and red-white oak. Most of the park's 223 acres is in the intermediate stage of succession, with small sections, such as the hemlock ravine, in the climax stage.

The park is as rich in history as it is in plant life. The stone walls lacing the park attest to the fact that, up to sixty years ago, much of this land was being farmed. Many of the hiking trails originated as wood-lot trails and roads. One such trail is on the west side of the Demonstration Gardens. It was a road at the time of the Revolutionary War and supposedly was used by British troops on their way to White Plains. The eastern end of the park includes an abandoned brick quarry; many arrowheads have been found in this area.

Although this park has been influenced by man throughout its history, today it is surprisingly isolated. Since it is not close to any town, it is practically inaccessible by public transportation. No train runs close enough to bring a taxi fare within reason. A bus line from Brewster does run near the park, but only on Saturdays early in the morning and late in the afternoon. For more information, call Walter's Transit at (914) 279-3354.

The best way to get to the park is by car. Take the Taconic State Parkway to the Route 134 (Kitchawan Road) exit and turn right. The park is 1.5 miles east of the parkway. A sign on the left marks the entrance. A short driveway leads to an ample parking area, where

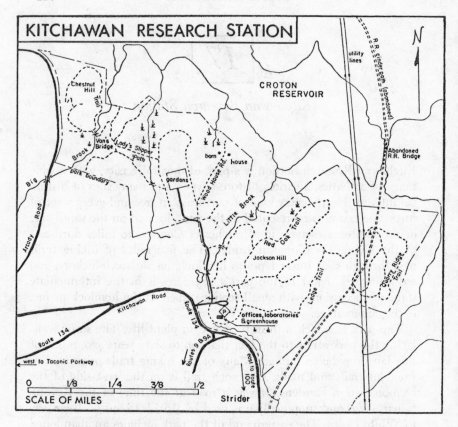

the trails begin. The buildings on the south side of the circle are the offices, laboratories, and greenhouse of the park. A pamphlet describing the park and including a map can be picked up at a small stand at the trailhead on the north side of the parking circle.

Though all the trails of the park are beautiful, the northwest corner is especially so. To get there, go north from the parking area on the long driveway to the Demonstration Gardens and take the path that starts on the western side of the gardens. This path, which takes a northerly direction, was the road supposedly used by the British troops during the Revolutionary War.

Soon arriving at a junction, turn left onto the Lady's Slipper Path. In May the lady's slippers will be in bloom. Two rows of red pines are to the right of the path. The trail soon swings to the north and then meets another trail. The path to the right, which we take, descends into Hemlock Ravine. The ravine is at its best in the winter, when snow clings to the evergreen branches. The trail makes an abrupt turn descending to the left and soon crosses Big Brook by Van's Bridge, a picturesque wooden structure. The bridge was named after the Van Brunt family, who donated this land to the park.

This is a good place to stop. The brook swings in a broad circle from beneath the trees, and then beyond the bridge it plunges over rocks into a ravine. With the sky peeking through the dense evergreen foliage overhead, the natural world seems very close and the modern world very far away.

Once across the bridge, take the trail to the right. Though the trail is a loop, it is easier to follow going this way. In general, this section is a little hard to follow. The Loop Trail circles Chestnut Hill, named for the vast number of chestnut trees that used to cover the hill and most of this area. Because of the chestnut blight, only stumps are left to remind us of this magnificent tree.

Take the trail back to the Demonstration Gardens. Situated in the middle of the park, the gardens were established in 1972. The five-acre site has exhibits which show various kinds of gardens and offer hints on how to improve your own garden. Among the exhibits are natural succession; different types of mulching; unusual vegetables; and weed identification. Each of the twenty stations in the Demonstration Gardens has an information booth which is filled with instructive pamphlets giving information on that exhibit.

After leaving the gardens, look for a path that goes northeast. This path leads to the Wood House, built in 1898. It was originally owned by Fernando Wood, once a well-known politician. In the 1920s it was bought by the Van Brunt family.

Fernando Wood was mayor of New York and then a United States congressman during the Civil War. Early in the war he achieved notice by proposing that New York City secede from the Union and declare itself a free port. Later he was one of the few in Congress to vote against the constitutional amendment ending slavery.

The house and the barn are still standing. Though the house has been vandalized, the barn is well preserved, and there are many antique toys and farm implements stored there.

Kitchawan

Another beautiful walk is the Little Brook Nature Trail. From the parking lot, go up the dirt driveway toward the Demonstration Gardens. Turn on the first path to the right, which crosses a brook and then follows it in a northerly direction. Along the trail are plaques identifying the ferns, plentiful in this area, and the trees. Little Brook Trail soon intersects the Red Oak Trail. The right fork returns to the parking area. Take the left fork, through the beech grove. Just beyond the grove is a tall and perfectly shaped oak that is approximately three hundred years old.

The Red Oak Trail continues in a northeasterly direction. Along this trail, as throughout the park, there are many stone walls left from the farming age. There are also many very old, large stumps along this path. Apparently the entire Jackson Hill area was logged at one time, leaving only the stumps of the huge primeval trees.

The trail circles around another striking hemlock forest, then passes a trail to the right that leads back to the research station. A little farther down, the Red Oak Trail passes another trail, the Ledge Trail, also on the right. The Red Oak Trail continues straight ahead, descending through a hardwood forest before crossing under a power line in a meadow. Once back in the woods, the trail crosses a cinder path, the remains of the railroad tracks of the old New York Central's Putnam Division. The path, used mostly by trailbike enthusiasts, leads back to Millwood on the south, passing under Route 134 and then crossing Route 100 on a still existing girder bridge. Northward the route continues to Mahopac; just a few paces north of the research station it crosses an arm of the Croton Reservoir.

Leaving the cinder path behind, the trail passes through an area that was once a brick quarry. Not surprisingly, there is a tremendous amount of rock here and also a stone wall. Many arrowheads have been found in this general vicinity. Eventually the trail loops back to the Red Oak Trail under the power line. Head back up the hill toward the research station. The first trail on your left is the Ledge Trail, which follows a ridge, then descends through a forest of primarily maple, oak, and ash before reaching the parking lot and research station.

The research station has pamphlets giving information on the park and the research done there. There is also a plant shop with many unusual house plants. It is open from 10 A.M. to 4 P.M. Tuesday through Saturday.

The laboratory of the research station was completed in 1959, with the greenhouse added in 1968. Topics studied include plant physiology, microbiology, plant pathology, plant breeding, and entomology (the study of insects). Current priorities include breeding magnolias and studying the various plant diseases caused by air pollution.

Courses are offered through the year at the station. They include collecting of insects, collecting and drying flowers, attracting wildlife to your garden, and drying fruit at home. Some of the courses meet only once, others as often as five times. For a calendar of courses, write the Kitchawan Research Station, 712 Kitchawan Road, Ossining, NY 10562, Attn: Education Department. The phone is (914) 941-8886.

Because the park is used for research and because some of the species there are on the endangered list, visitors are asked to observe some rules: no camping, picnicking, fishing, dogs or other pets. Wildlife and wildflowers and other plants should not be removed, and hikers should stay on the trails. The trails are not open to horses or motorized vehicles.

Even though the park is small, it is well worth going to. The hiking trails of the station are open every day of the year during daylight hours, and no admission is charged. Except for the Loop Trail at Chestnut Hill, the trails are easy to follow. With the range of activities available, a person or family can easily spend an entire day here, wandering and studying the natural world.

—STUART CHANDLER

Blue Mountain Reservation

Blue Mountain Reservation is located in the Hudson Valley on the outskirts of Peekskill. The park has sixteen miles of blazed trails. The hike described here is about six miles long.

The trails were built in the 1930s by the Civilian Conservation Corps (CCC). Some of them have not been worked on since, but the park maintenance staff is now in the process of rebuilding them. The orange and yellow trails at the beginning of this walk have recently been rebuilt and are in fine shape. The blue and red trails, the other trails used, still have muddy stretches where drainage is poor.

The entire walk is beautiful, passing through the rolling hills typical of the lower Hudson Valley. The trails, even where they have not been worked on, are broad and easy to follow. Hemlock groves and imposing rock formations are everywhere, particularly in the northern part of the park. The trails follow rivers, climb two mountains with views over the Hudson and Bear Mountain Park, and pass a large and attractive pond. Whether you are on the trails or in the recreation areas, the entire park is very clean and almost free of trash.

To get to the park by car, take Route 9 along the east shore of the Hudson to the Welcher Avenue exit, about 35 miles north of the George Washington Bridge. Turn east, away from the river, onto Welcher Avenue and follow it straight for about a quarter mile to the entrance of the park. At the entrance booth, a fee for parking may be charged, depending on the season. Just past the booth, the road forks. Go left to parking lot No. 3 and the trails.

To get to the park by train, take the Hudson Division to the Montrose station. From the station it is a two-mile walk or taxi ride to the park. The hike for the train users starts and ends at Montrose Station Road; otherwise the walk is the same.

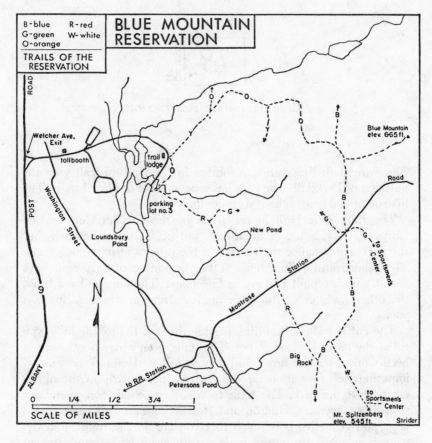

The 1,586 acres of Blue Mountain Reservation were originally owned by several families, and much of the acreage was farmland. Throughout the park are stone walls dating from farming times. The Montrose Reformed Church also owned part of the current-day park.

The Loundsbury family owned the hundred acres around Loundsbury Pond, where today the picnic areas and beach are located. The family operated a general contracting, sand, gravel, cement, brick, and ice company from their property. Both New Pond and Loundsbury Pond were originally constructed by the Loundsbury family specifically for making ice. For some reason, these ponds get much more ice than most others in the Westchester County area. For example, in the winter of 1977, when most ponds had only twelve inches of ice, Loundsbury Pond had twenty-five inches.

The gravel pit used by the Loundsbury Company was located at the site of the present-day parking lot for the beach. The red brick building to the right of the road just before the entrance to the park, the building now used by Tupperware, was once a stable for the Loundsbury Company horses. In the 1920s, when demand for ice lessened, the Loundsbury family sold their land to Westchester County.

In June 1933 the Civilian Conservation Corps (CCC) made the park into one of its camps. The CCC was an independent government agency inaugurated in April 1933 to help offset unemployment caused by the Depression. Its camp at Blue Mountain Reservation was one of fifteen hundred such camps throughout the United States. The two hundred men in the camp received room and board and were paid thirty dollars a month. If a man had dependents, he was required to send a minimum of twenty-two dollars of his pay to them.

The CCC at Blue Mountain Reservation built the fireplaces in the picnic areas, the two stone latrines near the park office, and the fire tower on Mount Spitzenberg, which was used as a ranger station for many years. Only the first story of this tower now remains. The CCC also built the lean-to on Blue Mountain, the sixteen miles of hiking and bridle trails, and the trail lodge.

The trail lodge originally housed many of the CCC workers and was going to be part of a chain of youth hostels envisioned by President Franklin D. Roosevelt. His plan fell through, and the lodge is now owned by the park, which rents it out to the public.

If your group wants to rent the lodge, which can handle as many as thirty people, contact the Westchester Parks Department at (914) 682-2621 for an application form. Reservations must be made at least forty-eight hours in advance. Blankets, pillows, and mattresses are included in the cost.

One of the interesting and beautiful walks in the reservation begins at parking lot No. 3. Just after the road enters the parking lot, a wide trail starts up a slope covered with hemlocks. A few paces later, the trail forks. Follow the orange trail, which descends toward the left to cross a stream.

The orange trail is short and well maintained. Along the trail are posts put up by the Westchester County Youth Bureau in 1977. Each of these posts is a station identifying the natural features nearby. (A guide book, available at the park office, describes in detail the plants at each station.) The trail passes sugar maple, yellow birch, and black birch (station No. 1), and maple-leaf viburnum, witch hazel, American chestnut, and blue birch (station No. 2). In the low area by the stream are found Christmas fern and silvery spleenwort (station No. 3), with spicebush, red oak, and dogwood at station No. 4 as the trail moves up to higher ground. Station No. 5 identifies a place where rocks and various boulders were deposited during the last glacial period.

On the hillside above the road the orange trail passes sycamore and beech at station No. 6 and a tulip tree and pignut hickory at station No. 7. Station No. 8, by a stone wall, marks shagbark hickory, as well as Virginia creeper and poison ivy. At station No. 9 is a white oak.

The orange trail returns to the road and ends at station No. 10—Eastern hemlock and white pine. Across the road is the trail lodge, a rambling low brown structure. Continue to the right on the well-maintained yellow trail. This trail gradually rises through a rocky, hemlock-choked gorge to a junction. Stay on the yellow trail, not crossing the footbridge to the left. The yellow trail curves a little to the right and then comes to another junction, at the base of a large, forked hemlock. Continue right on the yellow trail, which begins to climb in earnest.

In another quarter of a mile or so, the yellow trail reaches a pass. At the height of land, by a large and relatively bare rock, an orange trail forks perpendicularly left. Turn onto the orange trail, which is marked with square orange rectangles. It curves up and left into the rocks. The trail is rocky and rather torn up by horses, but it is still in good shape. It follows along a ridge crest and then drops down into swampy terrain, which is usually not too wet.

When the orange trail meets the blue trail, go straight ahead. Soon you will come to a junction, marked by three hemlocks growing together. The blue trail continues to the right. The trail to the left is a short but steep climb to the summit of Blue Mountain. The view from the summit into the gorge where the Hudson cuts through the Highlands is well worth the climb. Near the top, a faint, stone-laid trail curves right, leading to the summit itself, which is wooded, and to the trail shelter, which at this writing is roofless. The view is from the rock ledge to the left of the trail.

Return to the base of the mountain. Go left on the blue trail, ignoring the unmarked side trails that branch off the trail as it leads into the southern part of the reservation. There may be sounds of gunshots in the distance, off to the left; these come from the Sportsmen's Center, a gun and archery range in the southeastern corner of the park. The trail comes to a wide cleared swath in the woods; this is Montrose Station Road, a dirt road that crosses the park. Since cars can use this road, there is a litter problem here, especially beer cans. Continue around the *Phragmites* reeds; watch for the blue blaze painted on rocks, and pick up the trail on the other side of the road.

At a T intersection, the blue trail meets the white trail that leads to the summit of Mount Spitzenberg. Turn left here. Unlike Blue Mountain, Spitzenberg is an easy walk. The trail follows along a ridge until it reaches the mount, which is a rocky spur on the

Near the top of Blue Mountain

Hudson River Highlands from Blue Mountain: Dunderberg, left;
Anthony's Nose, right

ridge. Just before the summit the trail splits. The trail down to the left goes to the Sportsmen's Center. The gunfire from the center is thunderous at this point. Passage on this trail is not recommended. The trail to the right climbs steeply on a thirty-yard grand staircase of stones to the summit.

On the summit is the foundation of what used to be the ranger station. The interior of the tower is now a dumping place for cans and picnic litter. Otherwise the spot is nice. The view is to the west and south, over the Hudson and the villages along the river.

Retrace your steps to the blue trail and continue ahead. About a quarter mile later is a junction with a trail blazed with red marks. Take a sharp right onto this red trail.

The red trail recrosses Montrose Station Road and then leaves the high ground, descending to New Pond. At New Pond, a lovely lake which is reported to have good fishing, several unmarked side trails branch off and circle the pond. Many of these are not shown on any map. The trail follows along the south shore of the pond and then swings up along the west to cross the outlet stream on a culvert. Leaving the pond behind, the red trail continues to descend, passing a junction with a green trail before arriving back at parking lot No. 3 and the picnic area at Loundsbury Pond.

In addition to trails, the park has a wide variety of recreational facilities, including the trail lodge, the swimming beach, fishing and picnic areas, and the Sportsmen's Center. The center is open from the middle of April to the end of November, and provides archery, trap and skeet shooting, and small-bore, large-bore, and pistol ranges.

During the winter there's ice skating on Loundsbury Pond. Most of the trails, particularly the bridle trails, are suitable for cross-country skiing. The trails are not maintained or patrolled, however, so the park staff recommends them only for experienced skiers.

The hiking in general is very nice, and the only trouble is with the mosquitoes, which are at their worst in early summer. In the fall, when they have died off and the leaves are turning, the walking is fine, especially the beautiful view from Blue Mountain.

—STUART CHANDLER

ROCKLAND COUNTY:
The High Hills Call

North of New York and across the Hudson is the most mountainous terrain of the metropolitan area. The mountains nearest the city are Hook Mountain and High Tor. These are the northernmost outposts of the Palisades, which border the Hudson River from the Tappan Zee to New York Harbor before finally disappearing beneath Staten Island. The Palisades originated 180,000,000 years ago, when molten rock was forced under intense pressure between strata of sandstone and then, millions of years later, uncovered by erosion. (The Watchung Mountains in central New Jersey arose at the same time; there the molten rock flowed directly onto the surface of the earth.)

Farther into Rockland County is a much larger mountainous area. These are the fabled Hudson Highlands. Bear Mountain, Storm King, and Dunderberg Mountain rise abruptly over a thousand feet above the Hudson. Farther inland, streams rush through rocky gorges and lakes nestle below wooded slopes.

The Hudson Highlands are part of a larger range. Called by geologists the Reading Prong, the range is known by many local names: the Green Mountains in Vermont, the Berkshires in Massachusetts, the Housatonic Highlands in Connecticut, and the Ramapos in New Jersey. Sweeping through Rockland and Orange counties, these mountains are some of the oldest in North America; in fact, they are older than the continent itself. A billion years ago, sedimentary deposits were transformed by tremendous subterranean heat and pressure into today's gneisses, schists, and marble.

When the range was first raised, it soared upward for ten thousand feet or more. In the next few hundred million years, it was eroded, ground down, raised up, and ground down again, but the rock endured. Only a few thousand years ago the highest mountains were over three thousand feet high, but then the glaciers came.

The glaciers profoundly altered all of the landscape of this area. They dug out most of the lake basins in Rockland County and

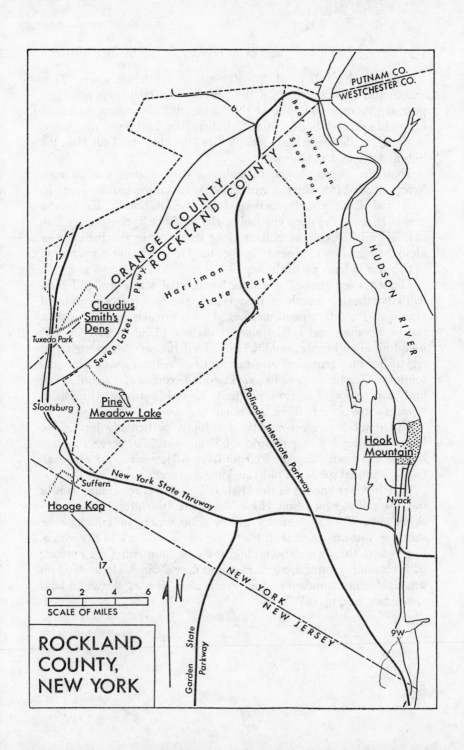

ROCKLAND
COUNTY,
NEW YORK

opened up the valleys of the Ramapo and Hudson rivers. They shaved two thousand feet off the peaks of the Highlands and then pushed this enormous pile of dirt south over the coastal plains of Long Island and Staten Island. Where the last wave of glaciers stopped, the dirt remained: today's Brooklyn Heights, Todt Hill, the hills in Alley Park in Queens.

Then the glaciers began to melt. As they melted, the sea rose. Water flooded into the low river valley between present-day Long Island and Connecticut, creating Long Island Sound. Salt water flowed back up the deep channel of the Hudson. Today the Hudson is tidal and brackish, as walkers along its shores in the Palisades or Hook Mountain will observe. In fact the Hudson is not a river at all in this area but an arm of the sea.

This complex geological history has created a multitude of local habitats: the salt marsh at Iona Island, the fresh-water swamps of Harriman Park, the ocean marshes of Cheesequake, barrier beaches, glacial moraines and kettle ponds, cliffs and plains—a diversity not found in any other metropolitan area. As if this weren't enough, this region lies in a transition area between two natural zones. Here the southern, Carolinian flora like sweet gum, persimmon, magnolia, and holly can be found in close proximity to such northern, Hudsonian types as maple, beech, birch, and hemlock.

The result is a great variety of wildlife, particularly birds. The Hudson Valley is a major corridor for the migrating species that will stop off at Jamaica Bay and Pelham Bay. In Harriman Park alone, almost a hundred species of birds are known to nest.

Walking is strenuous in the Highlands, but it is rewarding. Hawks ride the summer air below Hook Mountain. In winter, cross-country skiers glide through hemlock groves. The variety of fall colors is startling. But on a first visit, try to see Harriman Park in the spring. Everywhere the rhododendron and the mountain laurel are bursting with blossoms. Spring freshets roar, and deer abound. Henry Hudson was right, three hundred and fifty years ago: "It is as pleasant a land as one can tread upon."

Hook Mountain

The Hook Mountain circular walk is a varied and scenic exercise about four miles long, requiring two and a half to three hours to complete. The walk follows the cliffs of the northern extension of the Palisades, which fall off sharply to the Hudson. It wanders across pastures of lichens and wildflowers, through forests of box elders and hundred-year-old hemlocks, and then down to the water's edge and past abandoned rock quarries along the Hudson to the starting point.

Driving to the trail is not hard. Find Route 9W, the major highway running up the west side of the Hudson from the George Washington Bridge to the Bear Mountain Bridge and beyond. Hook Mountain is 20 miles north of the George Washington Bridge. Drive to Upper Nyack, a little north of the New York State Thruway, and look for an intersection with Old Mountain Road (sometimes called Christian Herald Road) on the right. This intersection will be found just before 9W starts to climb. Park in the open field on the left side of the highway, recross the highway, and pick up the blue blazes of the Long Path heading north along the road.

If possible, however, try to take the bus to this hike. It is an easy and convenient ride, and after the hike the bus rider has more freedom to explore in Nyack. Take the Red & Tan No. 9 from George Washington Bridge Terminal. Buses leave every hour at ten past the hour. Get off at the Old Mountain Road stop at Highway 9W.

Begin walking north up 9W; this is the direction where the highway soon starts to climb and curves to the right. Notice that on the telephone poles bordering the highway are blue paint markers; this is the Long Path. A few hundred feet farther along, a broad path slants off to the right. The blazes follow this path. The path follows the contour of the hill. This was once the route of the highway; the new

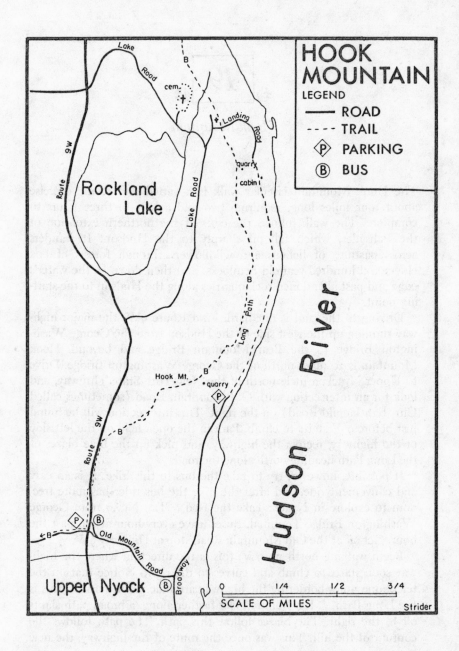

HOOK
MOUNTAIN
LEGEND
——— ROAD
- - - - TRAIL
Ⓟ PARKING
Ⓑ BUS

Lake Road

cem.

B

Landing Road

quarry

cabin

Route 9w

Rockland Lake

Lake Road

B

Long Path

Hudson River

Hook Mt.

quarry

Ⓟ

Route 9w

B

Ⓟ Ⓑ

B

Old Mountain Road

Broadway

Upper Nyack Ⓑ

0   1/4   1/2   3/4
SCALE OF MILES

Strider

route is already out of sight above the trail, although the cars can still be heard. To the right, a shaded, rocky slope quickly drops away; to the left, seventy-five feet up the hill, is the rock retaining wall for 9W. Then the trail jogs almost imperceptibly to the right and becomes rockier; if you stop and look, you can see the faint traces of the old highway curving off to the left. At the same time, the new highway overhead turns away, and the traffic noise gradually fades.

Soon after, the trail forks. The lower fork, which is blazed, is the easier walk—the upper has more ups and downs. After a few hundred yards the two forks rejoin. The trail is now climbing, swinging around to the left. The foliage, dense up to this point, begins to thin out, allowing views of the slope of Hook Mountain ahead and of the swimming pool and tennis court of a camp some two hundred fifty feet below. Finally the trail swings into a little sag, with Rockland Lake ahead in the distance but hidden except in winter; here the trail makes a sharp right and climbs steeply for a hundred feet or so, coming out on the bare rock top of Hook Mountain.

Hawks circle overhead here. Seven hundred feet below, the Tappan Zee Bridge spans the glistening Hudson. On the horizon are the towers of Riverdale and Manhattan. Just below, so close that you feel as though you are intruding, are the backyards of Upper Nyack. West are hills; through the trees to the northwest, Rockland Lake can be seen. Beyond the lake is the long curving ridge of the Palisades, with High Tor jutting prominently. The Hudson and the hills of Westchester County are visible over the low ridge to the northeast. (For a breath-taking view and a short walk, this is as far as you need to go; there are few better spots anywhere along the Hudson.)

The walk continues along the top of the ridge, with many more views, and then comes out into a bare area with a completely open view to the east. The view of a few minutes ago, from Hook Mountain, was awe-inspiring; this view is a little frightening. You are next to the edge, the upper rim of an old quarry. No trees are out there, no slope or bushes, just open air and a hundred-foot drop. Small children should be kept back. Even adults should approach with caution, since the rock here, while hard, is crumbly. No one should attempt to rock-climb here.

The trail goes up past the quarry and into the trees, letting your heart slow down a little. Ahead is a grassy knoll, the last of the open views. Hook Mountain is the round-shouldered rise just south. Nyack is now farther away; the feeling is quieter, more restful.

The trail now leaves the spectacular, if sometimes littered, Hudson views. Descending, it passes an unmarked trail to the right that heads steeply down the wooded slope. Soon after, at some ruins, the trail makes a sharp left. Another unmarked trail leads a few paces to the right past a concrete boundary marker to the last real view over the river.

The blue blazes now lead down, crossing an old woods road. Ahead, Rockland Lake can be seen through the trees. Then the woods road comes in again from the right and makes a switchback; the trail joins it, levels out, and heads north on a broad path with easy footing. Before long, another old road comes in from the left; the slope below the trail becomes steeper and more open, with trees far below and the sound of a spring.

The road begins to climb, gaining the top of a hemlock-clad ridge. Keep an eye out for the markers; the trail at one point here seems to go ahead, but the markers lead left, past a low concrete monolith. On the other side of this low hill is a clearing fringed by a variety of trees—cedar, pine, and hemlock. This is a sheltered spot to have lunch if the weather is cold.

On the far side the trail drops down through a grove of hemlock to a clove, which it crosses next to a causeway, and then passes by a dark pond.

Now Rockland Lake and its picnic areas are close, and on a busy day the shouts and radios of reveling picnickers below can be heard. The trail begins to descend, passing unmarked trails. One of these is the old route of the Long Path, abandoned because it was too steep. The slope is rocky, with few bushes but old tall trees, including a tulip tree that blossoms toward the beginning of May.

Just beyond the tree are two sets of very large foundations, which were part of the ice industry that flourished here years ago. Before the days of electric refrigeration, ice was cut from lakes and ponds along the Hudson and floated down to New York. Some of it was exported as far as the Caribbean. Rockland Lake ice was considered superior; and the ice houses here, along with a railroad branch, a cog railroad, and a boat landing, employed hundreds of men in season. All that is gone now, but until a few years ago the rotting remains of ice boats lay in the Hudson just offshore.

The trail makes a last turn and comes out on a road at a barrier. Off to the left is a firehouse. On down the road is Rockland Lake State Park. Ahead, just out of sight on the hill, is an old cemetery. The blue blazes continue north past the cemetery, traversing High Tor and Low Tor; ultimately the trail will cross Harriman Park and then the Shawangunks and finally the Catskills, ending at Windham High Peak overlooking the Mohawk River Valley.

This walk more modestly turns *right* and follows the road down to the Hudson. Note the ruins, especially to the right: the diagonal rock structure is a conveyor that once took ice down to Rockland Landing. A little farther down, this asphalt road—Ice House Road— passes the first of several abandoned quarries. The rock spires shoot up dramatically, and the columns from which the Palisades take their name are very visible here, but the whole prospect has a raw and man-made look about it.

Quarrying began here in the 1870s. Before long, thirty-two quarries were literally eating up these cliffs to feed rock to New York City's houses, roads, and office buildings. When it became apparent that the cliffs could disappear altogether, protests began; money was collected and bonds were sold to buy the cliffs and put them beyond the reach of the blasters. In 1911 the large quarry near the beginning of this walk was purchased; by 1920 the last quarry in this stretch passed into the hands of the state.

A dirt road winds off to the right, along the base of the quarries. The asphalt road seems at first to be heading straight into the yard of a private house, but this is the ranger's bungalow, and the road passes by it. Side paths now diverge north, to Haverstraw. Ahead, in the water, is the Rockland Lighthouse. Still descending, the road passes a fork to the right and then an abandoned comfort station. At the bottom, the asphalt becomes cinder. Jutting into the river is the remains of a landing. It's now a grassy, tree-shaded point—a good place to stop and eat when the weather is warm.

The trail back to Upper Nyack runs right along the river on a dirt and cinder road. Built in 1932 to connect the two ends of the park, the road makes for a somewhat sterile walk despite its water's-edge location. Still, the walking is easy, and the constant activity is entertaining. Bicycles and joggers pass continually. In winter, cross-country skiing is popular. (For families with young children, this stretch is a good walk in its own right. Come in from Nyack, driving north on Broadway to the end. This leads right into Hook Mountain State Park. Leave the car in the lower lot and walk north on this path.)

Notice the overhanging rock ledges. The soft red sandstone has been eroded right out from under the more durable rock overlying it. After about twenty minutes the road passes a roomy shelter constructed from rock. A little farther on there are some picnic tables with a fireplace, then a few old foundations, and finally more picnic tables that signal the end of the walk is near. Here are the park headquarters and other facilities, including a water fountain at the near corner of the headquarters building. To avoid a road walk out of the park, follow the lower paved parking area to the end, past the parking-lot entrance, then pick up a path up the hill. Turn left just before the path goes through a rock wall and out onto the road.

When you get out to the city street, the walk is over, but some good walking still lies ahead. The car drivers will turn right at the first street, Larchdale. Their next turn is a left at the entrance of the camp onto Midland Avenue. Look for a short cut to the right through the woods. This trail, marked with red paint splashes, leaves about fifty feet past the camp entrance and soon passes a man-made pond. It eventually ties into the Long Path, which can be followed downhill back to Route 9W and the car. Since this short cut is informal, it may have become overgrown, so if you don't find the trail, just continue on the street to the next right, going west back to Highway 9W.

Bus riders have a more interesting prospect. Rather than go back to the original bus stop, continue down Broadway into Nyack. Broadway leads past interesting old houses, in architectural styles ranging from *château phonie* to the white Victorians that so fascinated the American artist Edward Hopper.

The first bus stop on Broadway is at a little grocery on the right, just past a firehouse, but consider walking on into the business district. Nyack is notable for its many fine craft stores, particularly for stained glass and original oil paintings. When satisfied, pick up the New York bus at the stop on Broadway at Voorhis Avenue.

—SUSAN SALTMAN and WALT HOUCK

Pine Meadow Lake

From lovely Pine Meadow Lake, set in a nest of hills, runs a fast, deep stream. The stream winds its way down between steep hillsides, joins Stony Brook flowing out of Lake Sebago, and finally flows into the Ramapo River near Sloatsburg, New York. A trail follows the stream closely, leading the hiker to the waterfall and pool known as the Cascade of Slid. Another trail follows Pine Meadow Brook for a time, takes to higher ground above the Cascade, returns to the stream, and finally reaches Pine Meadow Lake.

The trail along the brook is very crowded in summer, so it is best enjoyed at another season. Snow permitting, it is good for ski touring and snowshoeing in winter, and lovely during the high-water times of spring and fall.

A walk up to the Cascade of Slid is recommended for people using public transportation to get to the park. This is a pleasant six-mile tramp (round trip) along the banks of Stony and Pine Meadow brooks. Allow five hours for the trip, and you will have time to splash your feet in the water if the urge strikes you. (Swimming isn't allowed.) The walking is very easy, with gradual climbs to the high point of six hundred feet, and with good footing except for a short stretch of rock scrambling at the Cascade.

To get to the trail, which starts near Sloatsburg, take the Short Line bus bound for Monroe or Newburgh from the Port Authority Terminal at Eighth Avenue and 40th Street. Before leaving, make certain that the bus passes through Sloatsburg. The trip takes a little over an hour. You will be let off in front of the Marine Midland Bank in Sloatsburg, but you must request the stop.

For those who can drive to Harriman, and for the ambitious, a hike up to Pine Meadow Lake is in order. This involves a six-mile walk rising five hundred feet from the parking lot to the lake, but it

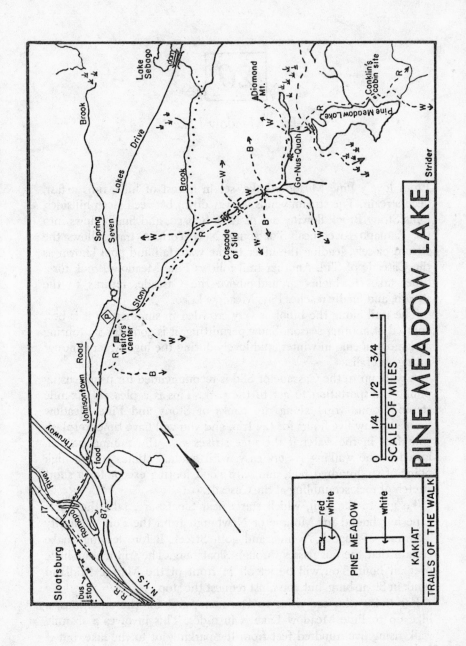

PINE MEADOW LAKE

Strider

SCALE OF MILES

0   1/4   1/2   3/4

TRAILS OF THE WALK

PINE MEADOW

● red
↓ white

KAKIAT

↓ white

is along or near Pine Meadow Brook most of the way. On reaching the lake, the hiker can walk along the shore to the site of the old Conklin cabin. Allow yourself six or seven hours and you will have time to explore the creeks, as well as the ruins along the lakeshore.

Either walking or driving, the instructions from Sloatsburg are the same. Total distance from the George Washington Bridge to the walk is 30 miles. From the Sloatsburg bus stop, proceed north on Route 17, soon passing on your right the Ramapo Valley Center Natural Foods Store. Along with good trail food, the store sells the New York/New Jersey Trail Conference maps of Harriman-Bear Mountain Park. The store is open seven days a week. Continue north on Route 17 to the top of the hill, turn right at the traffic light onto Seven Lakes Drive, and cross the railroad tracks on an overpass. At the bottom of the hill, you will cross the Ramapo River (a popular fishing spot) and soon pass on the left a restaurant where sandwiches can be bought.

After you've gone about two miles, a large clearing opens up on both sides of the road. On the right is a large building, the visitors' center, which at this writing is unstaffed. If driving, be sure to use the designated parking area. Cars parked on the shoulder may be ticketed. Plan on arriving early if you want to get a safe parking spot.

The hike leads from the right (east) side of the road. Follow the beaten path toward the woods. You will see a broad dirt track disappearing into the forest. This is the Pine Meadow Trail. The trees alongside are blazed with red dots on a white background.

Blazes provide a way of distinguishing one trail from another in a park that has many trails which merge and intersect frequently. They are painted on trees at eye level. When there are two blazes, one above the other, it means the trail is about to turn. Three blazes in a triangle, one above and two below, indicate the beginning/end of a trail. This system makes it very easy to follow the trail you want in most circumstances. There are times, however, when two trails marked in similar colors intersect or even run together. This is when having a map can be a big help.

The Pine Meadow Trail is marked in red, with white behind it to improve visibility. After entering the woods, ignore the white-blazed path (the Reeves Brook Trail), which goes off to the right. Follow the red, soon crossing a spring outlet and then passing a large, deep pool on your left. Follow this trail along the side of the creek for a half mile, passing groves of hemlock, laurel, and hardwood. At this point the Pine Meadow Trail branches off to the right. Go straight ahead on the left-hand, unmarked Stony Brook Trail. This broad and easily followed path stays by the creek.

Continue on the Stony Brook Trail until you come to a bridge across the brook to your left. Do not cross the bridge but follow the white blazes. After a short distance you will come to another bridge. Cross Pine Meadow Brook here and then immediately bear right. The trail is obscure here, so use caution. Climb into a gorge over large rocks, following Pine Meadow Brook on your right. This climb takes you to the Cascade of Slid, a beautiful waterfall and pool. This is a good spot for soaking tired feet and eating lunch.

After lunch, continue on the Kakiat Trail, the white-blazed trail you have been following. Soon you will pass a bridge (don't cross it) on your right and then cross the white-blazed Hillburn-Torne-Sebago Trail. Here the valley widens and becomes a bit marshy. Go straight on the Kakiat. After a short time pass on your left a cave up the hillside, where the blue-blazed Seven Hills Trail crosses the Kakiat. Follow the blue markers of the Seven Hills Trail, with the brook on your right. After a short distance the blue trail meets the red-blazed Pine Meadow Trail at a bridge.

Here you have a choice. The bus riders may wish to turn back here, since they have already walked two extra miles and have two more to get back to the stop in Sloatsburg. Other hikers will want to go on to the lake.

Those who are heading back to Sloatsburg should turn *right* on the red-blazed Pine Meadow Trail, crossing the bridge. After following the creek for a while, notice that the Hillburn-Torne-Sebago Trail (white-blazed) comes in on the left, coincides with the Pine Meadow Trail for a short distance, and then goes downhill to the right. Stay on the Pine Meadow Trail. You are passing the Cascade of Slid from high on the side of the gorge; it can be heard but not seen through the dense foliage. The trail crosses a cleared strip (gas line) and a brook. Shortly after, the unmarked Stony Brook Trail comes in on the right. From this point you are going back on the same trail you started on. Remember to turn left at Seven Lakes Drive and left again at Route 17. The bus stop is in town, at the lot across the street from the northbound stop. You will have to flag the bus to make sure it stops.

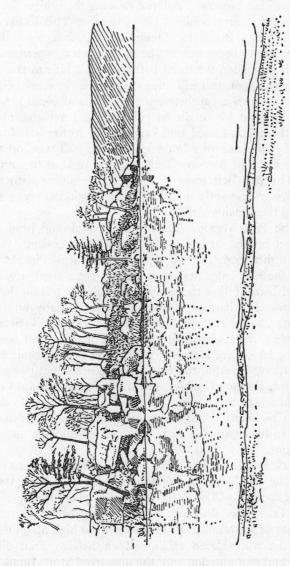

Pine Meadow Lake, Harriman State Park, New York

Those who decide to keep going up to the lake should turn *left* on the red-blazed Pine Meadow Trail, not crossing the bridge. Soon you will see some very large boulders on your right. This formation is called Ga-Nus-Quah Rock (the Stone Giant). Along with the red blazes, yellow blazes begin here at the rocks. Directly upstream from these rocks is a wonderful natural bathtub and a falls in the brook. After passing this spot, you will once again leave the creek below, as you head up through a gap between two hills and come to a clear area, with Diamond Mountain on your left and a marsh on your right. Here the yellow-blazed trail branches off to the left. Immediately beyond is the ruin of a building. A stone wall veers off to the right. Follow the Pine Meadow Trail and bear right at the next trail junction. (The path left leads to a concrete building with a roof showing above ground and the rest under it. Beyond are excavations, rockpiles, and the remains of a dam.)

Still on the Pine Meadow Trail, cross a creek and head uphill through laurel bushes. At the top of the hill you emerge from the woods onto a dirt road. To your right is the dam of Pine Meadow Lake. From the rock ledge next to it you can get a good view of the lake. The red blazes follow the shore of the lake for a short distance, then cut across the base of a small peninsula. Many faint trails branch off here, so use caution. Soon the Pine Meadow Trail returns to the lakeside and stays by it for half a mile or so, until it nears the far end of the lake. Here is the site of Conklin's cabin. Built around 1779 by Matthew Conklin, the cabin was occupied until 1930. The last inhabitant, Ramsey Conklin, was a great-great-grandson of the original builder. He was forced out when the lake was flooded by the Civilian Conservation Corps but continued to spend his summers in the area. In his eightieth year he disappeared into the mountains for the last time.

To get back to the parking lot on Seven Lakes Drive, turn back and follow the red blazes of the Pine Meadow Trail all the way down. This time you will cross the log bridge where the blue-blazed Seven Hills Trail joins. Bear left, still following the red blazes. You soon lose sight of the brook as you follow it from high up on the hillside. Cross the white-blazed Hillburn-Torne-Sebago Trail. Finally, you will descend to a junction with the unmarked Stony Brook Trail. This is the trail you came in on; follow it to Seven Lakes Drive. The bus stop is two miles down the drive to your left, as described above.

This is a walk for all seasons. In spring and fall the high water makes an endlessly fascinating spectacle as it rushes and flows over and around the rocky creekbed. In summer the water slows down and beckons from several excellent pools. Winter brings it almost to a halt, as the rocks are glazed with ice and the snow creates fantastic forms on the rocks it covers.

—BARBARA RODEKOHR

Thanks to Mr. Gardner Watts of Suffern for the historical information on the Conklins.

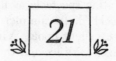

Claudius Smith's Dens

Within the boundaries of Harriman and Bear Mountain state parks, 51,000 acres of dense woodland and mountainous terrain have been preserved. The hiking trails, among them a section of the Maine-to-Georgia route of the Appalachian Trail, meander through intimate pine forests, follow the shores of quiet lakes, and climb to rocky peaks that afford panoramic views of the surrounding mountains and valleys.

The four-hour hike from Tuxedo Park up to the hideout of the notorious Revolutionary War bandit Claudius Smith follows a circular route of about seven miles in the southwestern part of Harriman Park, in the Hudson Highlands of Rockland and Orange counties, 30 miles northwest of the George Washington Bridge. Drivers can take Route 17 to Tuxedo Park. For users of public transit, the Short Line makes regular runs to Tuxedo Park from the Port Authority Bus Terminal. Buses leave at hourly intervals, following Route 17 north through New Jersey, and arrive in about an hour at Tuxedo Park, at the parking lot alongside the railroad station. Drivers may park here on weekends and holidays only.

The small cinder-block building directly across the highway is the pickup point on the return trip. This building also houses a pharmacy, lunch counter, and soda fountain; bus tickets can be bought here, although the round-trip ticket bought at the Port Authority is cheaper.

A short distance from the starting point of this hike is the site of the former Augusta Ironworks. An early guide described it thusly:

"a stone building 70 ft long with 4 fires and 2 hammers . . . on the ridge a cistern 70 ft long 8 ft deep and 10 ft wide kept full of water for extinguishing fires . . . anchor works makes 60 tons yearly & grain & saw mill belongs to this establishment (belonging to Sol Townsend)."

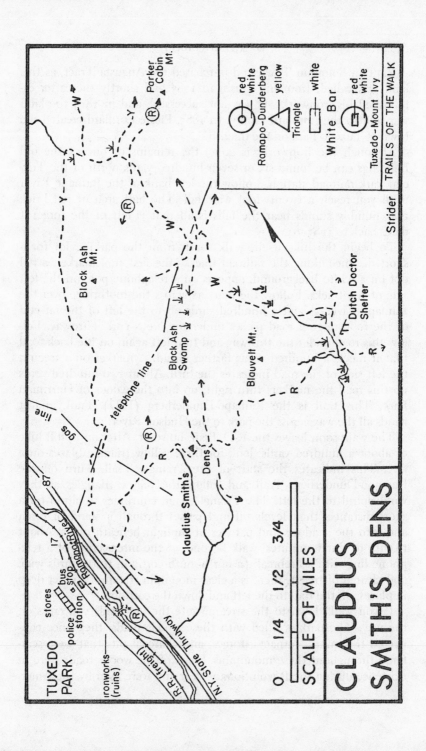

TUXEDO PARK

stores
bus stop
police station
Ramapo River

ironworks (ruins)

R.R. (freight)
N.Y. State Thruway

17

87

gas line

telephone line

Black Ash Mt.

Black Ash Swamp

Blauvelt Mt.

Dens

Claudius Smith's

Parker Cabin Mt.

Dutch Doctor Shelter

W

Y

Y

Y

W

W

R

R

R

R

R

R

TRAILS OF THE WALK

red
white   Ramapo–Dunderberg

yellow   Triangle

white   White Bar

red
white   Tuxedo–Mount Ivy

Strider

SCALE OF MILES

0   1/4   1/2   3/4   1

CLAUDIUS
SMITH'S DENS

Captain Solomon Townsend purchased the Augusta Tract, as this land was called, from his cousin in 1783 and shortly thereafter established his ironworks. It was not successful, and in 1814 the land was sold to the Lorillard family. In 1885, Pierre Lorillard created the town of Tuxedo Park on the tract.

Although the ironworks is gone, the remains of one of the old buildings can be found six or seven hundred yards north of the Tuxedo Park railroad station. Follow the left bank of the Ramapo River until you reach a twenty-foot waterfall. The half arch of red brick that humbly stands near the falls is all that is left of the forge; it dates back to 1783–84.

To begin the hike itself, walk south from the parking lot for a short distance along the railroad tracks—the first trail marker, a red dot on a white background, appears on a telephone pole on the left side of the tracks. Follow the markers across the footbridge over the Ramapo River. About a hundred yards off to the left of the far end of the footbridge a road passes under the New York Thruway. Follow this road under the thruway and turn left again on the back road that it meets a hundred yards farther ahead. A marker on a tree on the left side of the road indicates the turn. About two hundred yards up this road the markers turn right, up into the woods of Harriman Park. This trail is the Ramapo-Dunderberg (R-D) Trail, and it winds all the way across the park to the Hudson River.

The walk soon leaves the R-D Trail, however. After an uphill hike of about a hundred yards, look for three yellow triangle blazes on a tree. This indicates the start of the Triangle Trail. Turn off the Ramapo-Dunderberg Trail and follow the yellow triangles as they wind uphill to the left. The Triangle Trail continues to climb for a short distance, then levels off and passes through a stand of birch and into the shadows and patches of sunlight beneath pines. About twenty to thirty minutes' walk beyond, at the intersection of a telephone line with a firebreak (a north-south corridor, thirty yards wide and cleared of trees), there is a clear mountain stream, two feet deep in places, off the trail to the left and down the corridor.

If you walk down to the stream, note the old roads you cross on the way. The park is filled with these woods roads; they once connected the mines, furnaces, forges, and charcoal pits that were scattered throughout these mountains. Some of the woods roads were in existence during the Revolutionary War and were used by the Americans to transport munitions and supplies without risking British detection.

Returning to the trail, go another half mile, where the trail makes a sharp left, indicated by two blazes; here a woods road leads off to the right. A few hundred yards up this road, a vigorous stream shoots and spills down a path of stone ledges near the road—worth a short detour from the trail to see. Immediately following, the trail bends right and then leads through a passage where outcrops of stone rise twenty to thirty feet above the trail on both sides for about a hundred yards. Another mile ahead, the trail passes by a small swamp on the right, then climbs a slope for about a hundred feet, where it intersects the rectangular blaze of the White Bar Trail. (This was the route of the Long Path until 1981.) The two trails coincide for about a hundred yards, with a low ridge of outcropped bedrock on the left.

The large boulders that sit isolated on top of the ledge are "erratics," rocks that were picked up and carried along by glaciers. When the glacier melted, it set them here, far from the place of their origin.

Stay on the White Bar Trail as the Triangle Trail turns left toward Parker Cabin Mountain. Just a few hundred yards ahead, the White Bar Trail crosses the Ramapo-Dunderberg Trail. The terrain along the White Bar Trail continues level for a while, with a silhouette view of the distant mountains to the east. Then the trail descends for about a quarter mile into a valley, at the bottom of which is the extensive Black Ash Swamp.

The White Bar Trail crosses the swamp on a natural causeway, intersecting two other trails that also use the causeway. Then it climbs through thick bushes up the other side of the valley, the steepest climb of the day. The view from the top of the slope is magnificent: to the south, ahead in the direction you are walking, is Blauvelt Mountain, 1,177 feet high; to the northeast, behind you, is Parker Cabin Mountain, 1,200 feet; and to the northwest, so close that individual trees and rocks are discernible on its slope, is Black Ash Mountain, 1,044 feet. You might see hawks or turkey vultures circling between the mountains as they search for prey in the swamp below.

Descending for three quarters of a mile, the White Bar Trail winds around a patch of swamp, follows a dry stream bed of large boulders, and then circles to meet the end of the Triangle Trail,

Claudius Smith's Dens, after photo by Robert Cresko

which has swung back from Parker Cabin Mountain. Stay on the White Bar Trail as it turns right. About a hundred yards ahead, you will see the Dutch Doctor Shelter on the left, a short distance up the slope from the trail. Overnight camping is permitted in the open lean-tos, like Dutch Doctor, that are scattered throughout the park.

About fifty yards on the trail beyond the shelter there is a trailside stone fireplace and then an intersection with the Tuxedo-Mount Ivy Trail (TMI for short). The trail is blazed with a red *dash* on a white background—not to be confused with the Ramapo-Dunderberg blaze, a red *dot* on white.

Turn right, onto the TMI, which heads west toward Tuxedo Park. About a quarter of a mile ahead, opposite a small patch of marsh reeds, a thirty-foot-high outcrop of bedrock appears on the right side of the trail. Weathering has broken large chunks from its side to expose wavy bands of light and dark rock; these were once horizontal sedimentary strata subsequently twisted, bent, and hardened under tremendous compression.

One half mile on, immediately after intersecting the White Cross Trail, the TMI makes a sharp left and descends a narrow, rocky gorge. Just before you start down, you will see a blaze of the Blue Dot Trail (a blue dot on a white background) on a large boulder twenty-five yards straight ahead. If you walk out to the boulder you will find yourself standing on the edge of a cliff, overlooking the forest and hills stretching out in front of you like a carpet.

The TMI passes a small cave in the side of the cliff and another, larger one at the bottom. These cliffs, or overhangs, are known as Claudius Smith's Dens, after the rampaging bandit who used them as a hideout. From 1774 to 1779, Smith and his band of British sympathizers, among them his three sons, William, James, and Richard, terrorized residents of the Ramapo Pass. At first, as Loyalists, they stole only horses and cattle and sold them to the British troops, but later they raided homes and farms for whatever valuable booty could be had. They would sometimes burn the homes and murder the occupants. Following a night raid, the gang would return to the caves. The upper chamber was their hideout, while the lower was used to stable the stolen animals. This was only one of their hideouts; at other times they used Horse Stable Rock, about a half mile from Route 202 near Wesley Chapel. Eventually New York Governor Clinton offered a $500 reward for the capture of Smith. Since $500 in those days was a huge sum of money, Smith fled to Long Island and placed himself under British protection. There a supporter of the Revolution recognized him, formed a posse to capture him, and collected the reward. Smith was tried and, on January 22, 1779, hanged at Goshen, New York.

Smith and his band were not the first to use the cave for shelter. The Minsi Indians on their hunting expeditions returned every season to this and other protected campsites in the Highlands; pottery shards and arrowheads have been found nearby.

About a half mile farther on, the Tuxedo-Mount Ivy Trail ends at an intersection with the Ramapo-Dunderberg Trail. Take the Ramapo-Dunderberg left (west), and stay on it the rest of the way back to Tuxedo Park. The trail descends, then climbs to the left, passing an excellent viewpoint over the Tuxedo Park railroad station. From here the trail rapidly descends to the road, about thirty minutes' hiking time.

—KEN MULLEN

Hooge Kop and Bear Lake

The village of Suffern was known in colonial days as "Point of the Mountains." Today this remains an accurate description, since two major peaks of the Ramapos loom over the village, 25 miles northwest of the George Washington Bridge. Hooge Kop (High Head) lies a mile west of Suffern, astride the New York–New Jersey state line, and Noorde Kop (North Head) rises sharply from Wayne Avenue and the thruway. Both mountains may be explored by foot and offer the walker pleasant exercise, scenic beauty, and historical lore.

The Hooge Kop, also known as Houvenkopf Mountain, was once an extremely popular objective for hikers. The major road arteries since built at its base have complicated the access to its slopes. Hikers who come by car from the north on Route 17 will find a parking lot 2.1 miles south of the twin traffic lights at 6th Street in Hillburn (below the Motel-on-the-Mountain). The parking area is a section of old cement road off to the side of Route 17 just after the first thruway sign at the right of the road. Lock cars. Since Route 17 is divided here, drivers coming from the south should continue as far as the twin lights in Hillburn and turn around to approach the parking area from the north.

Bus access is possible, although more time-consuming. Take the Short Line coach from the Port Authority Terminal. Get out at the Suffern stop just before the thruway overpass and cross the railroad tracks near the brick police station. Follow the path down to the town baseball field and then take the dirt road past the first-base side of the field to the railroad spur. Continue along the railroad as it crosses the Ramapo River; then leave the tracks at the power line. Follow the dirt road under the power line and continue out to Route 17. Occasional yellow blazes help in finding the direction. Use caution in crossing Route 17 and then walk single file a quarter mile

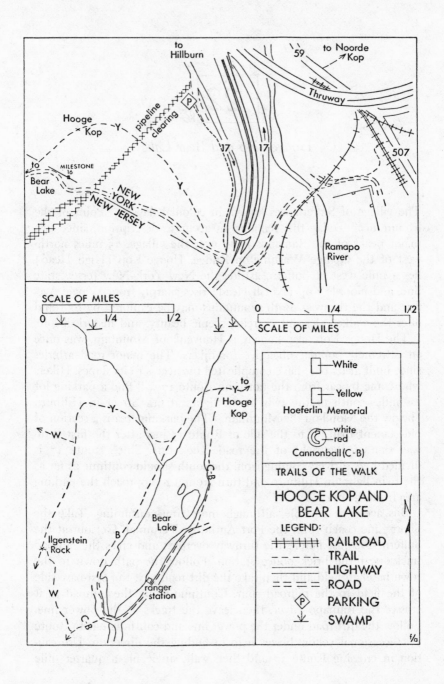

to Hillburn

to Noorde
Kop

59

Thruway

Hooge
Kop

Y

pipeline
clearing

P

17

17

507

to
Bear
Lake

MILESTONE
16

NEW
YORK

NEW JERSEY

Y

Ramapo
River

SCALE OF MILES

0   1/4   1/2

0   1/4   1/2

SCALE OF MILES

White

Yellow

Hoeferlin Memorial

white
red

Cannonball (C-B)

TRAILS OF THE WALK

HOOGE KOP AND
BEAR LAKE

LEGEND:

to
Y

to
Hooge
Kop

Y

W

C-B

Bear
Lake

B

Ilgenstein
Rock

ranger
station

W

C-B

RAILROAD

TRAIL

HIGHWAY

ROAD

P PARKING

SWAMP

N

1/a

north on the shoulder of the highway to the paved strip where the walk begins.

From the paved strip it is a three-quarter-mile walk and a climb of 450 feet to the summit of Hooge Kop. At the very beginning of the pull-off area, before the pavement starts, begin a steep climb up the gas pipeline clearing. Pause for a rest at a crest of the hill before descending to a seldom-used paved road. Now follow this road uphill, to the right, but eliminate the bend by taking an unmarked path to the right. Just before rejoining the road, note on the right side of the path the sixteenth of the milestones marking the border between New Jersey and New York. The dull red blazes on some of the trees are old survey marks indicating the state line.

The road passes some cabins. Soon after reaching a crest in the road, the walker should be alert for the yellow trail that ascends the back of the Hooge Kop. A short and easy climb leads to the summit and to gigantic Split Rock. The rock, also called Camp Meeting Rock or Pigeon Rock, has a long history. A century ago the mountain people scattered grain on the flat area around the rock and netted the then numerous passenger pigeons as they landed. In the 1920s the slope below the rock was the occasional scene of a strange and sinister event: the Knights of the Ku Klux Klan, then strong in New York and New Jersey, burned large fiery crosses on the mountainside. These demonstrations were easily visible in Suffern.

The rock itself can be climbed, most easily through the wide crack from the west side. The beautiful panoramic view from the top of the rock takes in Suffern's business district, schools, churches, and major roads, as well as the surrounding countryside and the hills of the Ramapos. On clear days the skyscrapers of New York City are visible.

The huge building at the base of the hill was the Ford Company's assembly plant in Mahwah. Built in the mid-fifties, the now closed plant replaced a small airplane field and the Houvenkopf Country Club. On the slope south of Hooge Kop, toward Stag Hill, is a small dammed lake created in the 1920s to supply water to the eighteen-hole course. This pond was a favorite spot of noted local hiker William Hoeferlin and his friends. Hoeferlin, whose hiking maps are still in wide use, had his cabin, Bluebird Lodge, located near the gas pipeline below Split Rock.

Now look northwest, up the Ramapo Valley toward Hillburn. In the summer of 1777, Washington and his 8,000-man army spent a week here prior to their march to Philadelphia and the Battle of the Brandywine. The "Post at Sidman's Bridge" was an important garrison during the war, blocking British forces that threatened to break into the Ramapo Valley and come up from behind on the American forts on the Hudson.

Looming over Hillburn is the Ramapo Torne. About 1,200 feet in elevation, it is the mountain with bare, reddish-yellow cliffs about two miles north of the Hooge Kop. Several Indian rock shelters have been discovered on its slopes, including one that has yielded more than two hundred artifacts. During the Revolution the Torne was an American sentinel post. Local tradition has Washington himself climbing the Torne in July 1777 to scout for the tall masts of the British fleet in lower New York Harbor. Below the Torne is a huge electrical substation, breaking the isolation of the once remote Torne Valley. The summit of the Torne and the wild areas to the north and east of it can be explored using trails in Harriman Park.

Just to the northeast of Hooge Kop is the beginning of the Ramapo Clove, the major route through the mountains. Note the nar-

Suffern, Bluebird Lodge, after photo by Nat Lester

rowness of the Clove; during colonial days, before earthmovers and bulldozers, there was scarcely room between the pressing hills for the Ramapo River and the old Orange Turnpike. Beyond the Clove rises Noorde Kop. The slopes of this mountain show signs of man's presence. John Suffern, founder of the village of Suffern, had potash works up there almost two centuries ago. Dating from the nineteenth century are more pits—rectangular sunken depressions where charcoal burners and woodcutters created charcoal for the flourishing iron industry.

From Split Rock, hikers may be seen on Noorde Kop, sometimes called School Mountain. The yellow-marked Suffern-Bear Mountain Trail ascends Noorde Kop steeply from Route 59 a fraction of a mile north of the village. Cars can be parked under or near the thruway bridge. The yellow blazes begin in the right a little north of the bridge. These blazes continue all the way to Bear Mountain, twenty-four rugged miles and a day's walk away. (The record time for the walk is five hours, forty-two minutes, set many years ago by a member of the City College Hiking Club.) A shorter walk can easily be fashioned. Continue past the rocky outlook at the summit. After the power line clearing, the yellow trail descends sharply, passing a long-abandoned woods road. This woods road turns sharply to the left (west). The road and then a small brook lead down to the circle of houses in East Hillburn on Route 59. This is just a half mile north of the trailhead near the thruway bridge.

Now leaving Split Rock, the hiker may continue the walk or return to the car. To return to the car, continue on the yellow trail that descends steeply off the Hooge Kop. When the trail crosses the pipeline clearing, return to the car via the clearing or stay on the yellow trail down to Route 17 and turn left a quarter mile to the paved strip and car.

The walker may choose to continue exploring westward after visiting Split Rock. The yellow trail goes all the way through the Ramapo Mountain State Forest (see walk No. 23) to Pompton Lakes, eleven miles south, but a more comfortable target for a day walk is Ilgenstein Rock, a round trip of about three hours. Backtrack off the Hooge Kop on the yellow trail, turning right when the road is reached. The yellow trail, once the Suffern-Midvale Trail and now officially the Hoeferlin Memorial Trail, follows roads for about a mile to the mountain community clustered around Silver Lake on

Stag Hill Road. Some of the houses here are new; others have been lived in for generations. The residents have diverse backgrounds. Some are descended from ancestors, black or white, who went into the Ramapos before the American Revolution. Others claim Indian lineage. A few new residents have come into the area in recent years.

Westward from Silver Lake the trail follows grassy woods roads built during the charcoal-industry days of a century ago. The hiker nearing Bear Lake (sometimes called Bear Swamp Lake) may feel with assurance that he or she is following the legendary Cannonball Road. This was a secret military highway used by American soldiers to transport weapons and munitions whenever the Valley Road (now Route 202) was not secure.

The trail forks at Bear Lake, with the red blazes of the Cannonball Trail diverging east (left). Continue to follow the yellow blazes right, past the intersection with the blue-blazed shore trail that circles the west side of the lake. The yellow trail climbs to the top of the hill above the lake, soon passing the water-filled pits of the Butler iron mine, which was worked during the Civil War. Soon after, a white-blazed trail comes in from the right. This side path connects with the trails in the Passaic County part of Ringwood State Park.

The yellow and white blazes run together as far as Ilgenstein Rock, a ledge overlooking the southern end of Bear Lake. From this point it is possible to make a loop around the lake by following the white blazes down to the Cannonball Trail and then turning left (north) on the Cannonball Trail along the lake shore to the intersection with the Hoeferlin Trail at the northern end of the lake. The hiker can now retrace his or her steps back to the Split Rock area, going the rest of the way down via either the road, the yellow trail, or the gas pipeline clearing.

—GARDNER WATTS

NORTHERN NEW JERSEY:
Soil That Was Indian

After the last glacier retreated, the first settlers began to arrive in what is now the metropolitan area. Various Indian tribes settled Long Island. The Wappinger Confederacy eventually gained control of the east bank of the Hudson. West of the Hudson dwelt the Leni-Lenape, "original people." The Leni-Lenape nation was made up of smaller groups; the group in northern New Jersey and nearby New York were the Minsi, "people of the stone country."

The Minsi recognized no central authority. Each settlement was self-governing, with its own defined areas for farming, hunting, gathering, and fishing. Permanent villages of sixty to a hundred inhabitants dotted the lowlands, particularly the Passaic River basin. Maize, beans, and squash were planted in nearby fields. In spring and summer small groups left the villages to live and fish along the rivers.

After the fall harvest hunting bands would head into the hills. Often they would return year after year to the same shelters to hunt and, in bad weather, to work on stone implements. In spring the bands would return to the lowland villages to help with the planting and farming.

Over three hundred and fifty generations the Minsi had evolved a stable lifestyle, one that ensured their existence by preserving the environment that made their existence possible. Then the Europeans came. They drove the Leni-Lenape westward, out of this area. Then they began to build. In the short span of fifteen generations, the plains and lowlands have been buried under landfill, roads, homes, factories, dumps, and shopping centers.

For a time, development also seemed to be the fate of the hills. The rock was rich in iron ore. The ore was magnetite, which was so concentrated that it could easily be smelted with eighteenth-century technology. By the time of the Revolutionary War the Highlands and Ramapos were producing fifteen per cent of the world's iron.

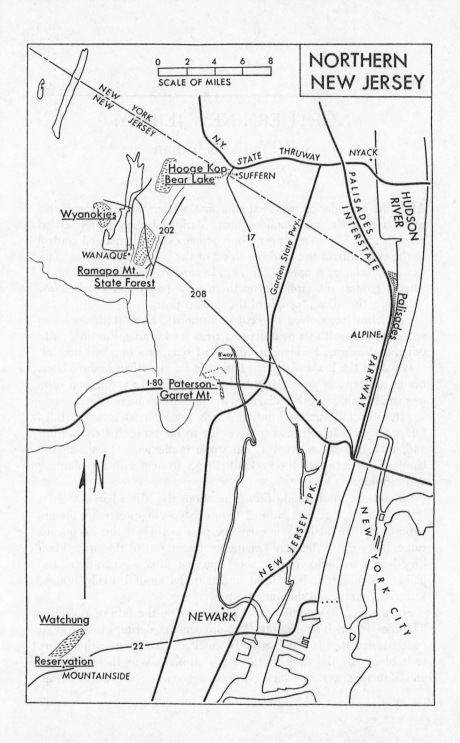

NORTHERN
NEW JERSEY

SCALE OF MILES
0 2 4 6 8

NEW YORK
NEW JERSEY

N.Y. STATE THRUWAY

NYACK

Hooge Kop
Bear Lake

SUFFERN

Wyanokies

202

17

WANAQUE

Ramapo Mt.
State Forest

208

Garden State Pkwy.

PALISADES INTERSTATE

HUDSON RIVER

Palisades

ALPINE

B'way

1-80   Paterson-
Garret Mt.

4

PALISADES PARKWAY

N

NEW JERSEY TPK.

NEW YORK CITY

Watchung

NEWARK

22

Reservation

MOUNTAINSIDE

Roads were built throughout the hills. Forests were decimated for the production of charcoal. Streams were dammed and canals dug for water.

Iron mining continued strong right through the Civil War in the 1860s. However, the opening of the Erie Canal and then the coming of the railroad meant that the poorer but much more abundant ores of the Midwest would gradually replace Highland iron. By the beginning of the twentieth century most of the Highlands were reverting to forest. Much of it passed almost painlessly to state ownership. In New Jersey the ironmaking families donated the Wyanokie plateau to the public. In New York a gift from the estate of railroad financier E. H. Harriman formed the nucleus of Harriman-Bear Mountain State Park.

So the mountainous areas, at least, are near to the condition in which the Minsi left them. Still, they are not safe from development. The Ramapo Mountain State Forest is seen as a fine potential route for Interstate 287. The Watchung Reservation lies conveniently in the path of Interstate 78; only continual community action has saved the reservation thus far from the fate of Van Cortlandt Park.

If you should go to Watchung Reservation, think about that as you stand in the quiet of the Glen. Consider the effect of 65,000 vehicles a day passing perhaps half a mile up the Blue Brook, just on the other side of Surprise Lake. And then think about the names of these places. So often they are the old Minsi names. Watchung means "hill" in the Algonkian dialect spoken by the Minsi. Ramapo is "place of the slanting rock." Wyanokie means "place of the sassafras"; Wanaque is another spelling of the word. Even Windbeam Mountain has an Indian root; it comes from *wimbemes*, or "lone tree mountain." There is no word for "highway"; let there be no highways among these hemlock-clad ravines, quiet meadows, and clear, singing cascades.

Ramapo Mountain State Forest

From north to south, the 2,340-acre Ramapo Mountain State Forest extends over six miles between Pompton Lakes and Oakland. Elevations range from 200 to 1,100 feet of rugged mountain terrain, with Ramapo Lake (elevation, 550 feet) as the centerpiece. Fishing is permitted at the lake, but swimming is not. Public access to the state forest is by foot only. The only roads still maintained give access to private inholdings in the southern part and to the District Ranger Station on the west shore of Ramapo Lake.

The trails in the state forest were planned by Frank Oliver, as a member of the New York/New Jersey Trail Conference, and were cleared by high school students in the Youth Conservation Corps during the summers of 1977 and 1978. The trails have been laid out to provide gradual ascents to rocky ledge viewpoints from which the land may drop off sharply. Two are loop trails, and two others are through trails.

One of the through trails is an old Conference path. Originally called the Suffern-Midvale Trail, it has been renamed the Hoeferlin Memorial Trail in memory of a famous trail blazer and mapmaker. At Matapan the former route to Midvale has been abandoned and a new route created to West Oakland.

Another through trail is the rediscovered historic Cannonball (C-B) Road. The road originated at Pompton Lakes, where there was an iron furnace predating the American Revolution. To avoid interception by the British, cannonballs were transported by wagon northeast behind the sheltering Ramapo Mountains.

Hiking can be done throughout the year. In the section south of Skyline Drive, hunting is prohibited because of the private inholdings. The deteriorated estate roads can serve as ski-touring routes in winter. Trail bikes are prohibited in the park, and no fires or camp-

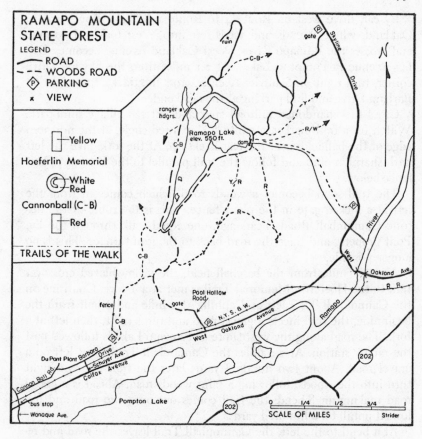

ing are permitted. Hikers are asked to bring out any trash they may come across.

There are a number of access points to the trails, but only one of these—at the southern end—can be reached by a short walk from public transportation. From the Port Authority Bus Terminal, the Warwick Division of the Maplewood Equipment Co. serves a stop at the former railroad station on Wanaque Avenue in Pompton Lakes. This same stop is served by Transport of New Jersey from Paterson (No. 86) and from Newark (No. 114). Cross the tracks and go north on the blacktop Cannonball Road, paralleling the tracks. Turn right on Du Pont Lane. The second left then leads to Barbara Drive. The trail starts at the dead end.

By car, drive west on Route 4 to Route 208. Take Route 208 to Oakland, where it ends and feeds left into West Oakland Avenue and crosses the Ramapo River. West Oakland Avenue becomes Colfax Avenue in Pompton Lakes. At 2.1 miles from the Skyline Drive corner, turn right on Schuyler Avenue, cross the tracks, turn right on Barbara Drive and find parking at the dead end.

Cross the abandoned railroad spur and enter a village mini-park. Watch for a trail marker, a white "C" in a red circle, at the northern edge of the ballfield, near the rear backstop. At the fork, take the left path sharply uphill and follow the trail parallel to the Du Pont plant fence below.

The trail soon becomes a woods road, which comes in from the left at a locked gate in the plant fence. This is the route of the historic Cannonball Road. Years ago, one could walk through the Du Pont property and trace the road back to the iron furnace. This is no longer possible.

About a mile from the baseball field, the yellow-blazed crossover trail to the Hoeferlin Memorial Trail is met at a Y-fork. Continue on the Cannonball Trail left and uphill. At a mile and a half from the beginning, the trail meets a gravel road and turns right, then left at a fork. The road along the west shore of Ramapo Lake is followed past the ranger station. At 2.2 miles the Cannonball Trail turns left on a gravel road. About two hundred yards later the trail makes a right turn into the woods, following a faint woods road. Ahead is a gravel road making an S-bend; the trail comes out onto the road and follows it uphill for a hundred yards.

At a bend to the left, the Cannonball Trail leaves the road and reenters the woods, soon crosses a stream, and heads northeast uphill on an easy grade. At the top the trail crosses a blacktop access road diagonally and parallels it north through the woods. The trail breaks out into a large field, then uses the road past a private home before entering the woods again. It rejoins the road just short of a gate and crosses Skyline Drive at the county line.

North of the drive, the trail follows an ancient woods road. In two hundred yards, the yellow blazes of the Hoeferlin Memorial Trail come in from the right. These two trails head north from here, the Hoeferlin going all the way across the New York State line to Suffern. This hike, however, turns to the right and onto the Hoeferlin Trail heading southeast, bringing the walker to a parking lot after a third of a mile. This lot is on Skyline Drive, 1.1 miles west of the intersection with West Oakland Avenue; it is an alternate access point to the Ramapo Mountain trails. Hikers with two cars may want to arrange to have one car left here. When they reach this point, they will be able to drive back, rather than walk, to where the first car was left.

But if the car was left at Barbara Drive or the hiker arrived by bus, alternate return hikes are possible.

An easy route back to Barbara Drive is to follow the Hoeferlin Trail to the outlet dam of Ramapo Lake. From that point, use the gravel road on the east shore of the lake. Keep left at the fork at the bottom of the lake and in a quarter of a mile watch for the yellow blazes of the Hoeferlin Trail as it emerges from the woods. The trail and road descend in a series of S-turns. After leaving an open area, watch for a woods road at right. This is the crossover trail, marked in red, that connects with the Cannonball Trail two hundred yards ahead. Turn left for Barbara Drive. The gravel road continues down to a car parking lot at Pool Hollow Road, the southern terminus of the Hoeferlin Memorial Trail. If you missed the crossover trail, follow the path to the right along the railroad back to the mini-park at Barbara Drive.

A more scenic, but more strenuous, return trip would be to continue on the yellow Hoeferlin Trail past the dam. Around a bend, the trail leaves the road and climbs a rocky ridge with three wide lookouts. A third of a mile farther, the trail climbs a rocky pinnacle overlooking Ramapo Lake. A second lookout amid scrub pine comes up after another third of a mile. Dropping down the rocky ledge, the trail reaches another lookout and then descends to a brook. Climbing, it reaches a gravel road swinging in from the right. To return from here to Barbara Drive, follow the directions in the paragraph above.

For the longest but most scenic return route, follow the Hoeferlin Trail back to the dam. The red Lookout Trail takes off from the south end of the dam (look for three red markers) and proceeds down the south side of the outlet brook. It soon climbs about two hundred and fifty feet to two rock ledge viewpoints about a mile from the dam. The second is downhill from the first. From the second, backtrack four hundred feet to a Y-fork, where the left branch of the trail heads west to a large stone marking the property corner.

Ramapo Lake from Hoeferlin Memorial Trail

From here the trail heads south to a rock ledge with views west toward the Wyanokies, where the red Lookout Trail joins the yellowblazed Hoeferlin Trail. The red blazes coincide with the yellow going north, as the red trail makes a loop back to the dam. Follow the yellow blazes south, following the directions above, to return to Barbara Drive.

Ramapo Mountain State Forest is a recent addition to New Jersey's public lands. The tract had been the estate of Oakland Mayor Clifford F. MacEvoy, a wealthy contractor of large public works, including the Wanaque Reservoir. The former estate roads are being allowed to deteriorate, with short sections used for marked trails.

The main hike described here will serve as an introduction to this new hiking area. For returning hikers, the combinations of trail and road make possible a variety of walks—from short strolls along level roads to lengthy exercises over rocky ledges and crests.

—FRANK J. OLIVER

24

Wyanokies

Route 4 in New Jersey runs west from the George Washington Bridge through pleasant suburbs and past busy shopping malls. Before long it forks; the right fork, Route 208, is more pleasant yet, but still suburban. At the town of Oakland, Route 208 feeds into Skyline Drive, which passes through woods as it goes up and over an arm of the Ramapos (the sharp-eyed may spot the Hoeferlin and Cannonball trail crossings at the top of the ridge). Skyline Drive then dips down again into a valley and passes more suburbs and a large shopping center.

Where Skyline Drive ends at Route 511, a left turn onto Route 511 (Ringwood Avenue) soon takes the driver along the shore of the Wyanokie Reservoir, which has substantial hills on its far side. Then the road curves away from the shore, past a gas station and stores. An unmarked side street goes off to the right and over a little rise. Ahead on that road is a small patch of true wilderness.

On the other side of the rise, the Wyanokie Reservoir stretches north and south, an alpine lake surrounded by high hills (ahead is the highest, Windbeam, at 1,100 feet; there's a trail over it, but not the trail for today). The road narrows, crosses a long, ancient white bridge, and then clings to the hillside just above the reservoir.

At the end of an arm of the reservoir, West Brook Road comes to a fork. Go left. Ignore the first road to the left and take the second, which is Snake Den Road, then take two more lefts on this road, until it passes a parking lot on the right. The sign says, "Weis Ecology Center."

Fifty years ago this area was all wilderness. Wrote a delighted hiker at the time, "There are nearby areas in New Jersey that are too wild and too worthless to be taxed and . . . within these areas it is possible for a man to get thoroughly lost while still in sight of the

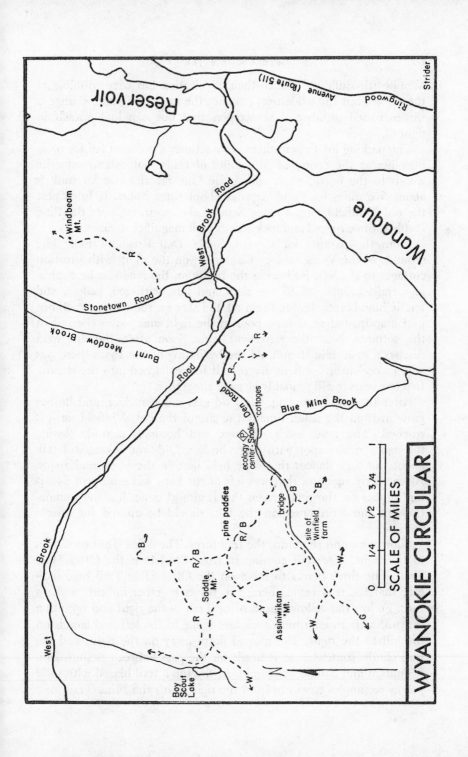

WYANOKIE CIRCULAR

SCALE OF MILES

0   1/4   1/2   3/4   1

Reservoir

Wanaque

Windbeam Mt.

West Brook Road

Stonetown Road

Burnt Meadow Brook

Den Road

Blue Mine Brook

cottages

ecology center snake den

pine paddies

site of Winfield farm

bridge

Saddle Mt.

Assiniwikom Mt.

Boy Scout Lake

West Brook

Ringwood Avenue (Route 511)

Strider

Woolworth Building." Since then, civilization has been nibbling at the woods, but the wilderness remains; the most noticeable change is the increased number of skyscrapers that one can lose oneself in sight of.

The parking lot (where there is sometimes a nominal fee for parking) lies at the center of fifty miles of trails that extend into the woods to the north, west, and south. One favorite circular walk is about five miles long and requires about three hours. It leads past the old Winfield farm to Boy Scout Lake, returning over the Pine Paddies, three rugged and rocky crests with magnificent views.

From the parking lot stay on Snake Den Road on foot. The grounds of the Weis Ecology Center are on the right, with vacation cottages to the left. Following the blazes on the road can be confusing: trails branch off to the right and left, with red, yellow, and finally blue blazes. Ignore them all and stay on the road as it climbs past a spring-fed swimming pool to the right and passes the last of the cottages. Now the pavement ends. Soon after, the dirt road reaches a mountain stream. At the beginning of the 1970s there was still a wooden bridge here. By 1980 it had collapsed into the stream. In a few years it will probably be gone altogether.

After the brook crossing, the road gets much rockier, and bushes grow in from the sides. Finally the site of the old Winfield farm is reached. The road levels off here and becomes a trail, passing through a grassy spot with berry bushes. Old-time hikers still talk about the barn dances that were held here in the 1930s and 1940s. By the early 1970s all that was left of the barn was a heap of decaying lumber on the right. Even this is almost gone, but the foundations of the farmhouse, on the left, should be around for several years yet.

Shortly beyond the farm, the trail forks. The Mine Trail continues to the right. The trail coming in from the left is the Otter Hole Trail. The three blazes together on the Otter Hole Trail here indicate that the trail begins here; two blazes together indicate a sharp turn. Follow the yellow-blazed Mine Trail to the right and up into a canyon, with an enormous rock face rising to the left and laurels on the hill to the right. The ground drops away on the right, and the trail climbs somewhat as it heads for the pass between Assiniwikam Mountain and Saddle Mountain. At the top a trail blazed with solid yellow rectangles comes in from the right, joins the Mine Trail for a

few paces, and leaves to the left. The yellow dots of the Mine Trail
continue through clumps of laurel.

Where the trail begins to descend, the Stone Hunting House Trail
(white) comes in from the left and ends. Ahead on the Mine Trail is
a stretch of several hundred feet that is usually wet. Boulders and
fallen logs give dry passage to the sure-footed. The blazes here are
sometimes hard to spot, but the trail continues straight ahead. Cross
a stream on a log; beyond, the trail goes up a little and dries out, as
the first of the shelters at Boy Scout Lake comes up. (These shelters
are owned by the Scouts and are not available for public use.) Boy
Scout Lake is a pleasant pond and no more than that, but the dam
at the northern end is a warm and dry spot to eat. Continue along
the path, which runs a little distance from the lake, crossing an inlet
stream on a rude plank bridge. Just before the dam, look for a trail
blazed with a red dot on a white background; this is the trail from
the dam after lunch.

The dam is a sleepy spot. The sun warms the concrete, the water
slaps lightly below, and clouds drift over the trees. In a time-honored
tradition of club walks, this is a good time and place to relax and tell
a story.

In the 1800s the Wyanokies were mined for iron. Mines can still
be seen in the woods today; two are located a little south of where
this walk started. The forge in the vicinity, Freedom Furnace, could
still be explored in the 1920s; today it is under the waters of the
Wanaque Reservoir. The Ringwood Mining Company logged these
thousands of acres west of the reservoir to provide charcoal for the
furnace. Most of this land was never farmed; the stone fences that
can be found in so many of the woods of the northeast are not often
found in the Wyanokies.

After the last mine shut down, in 1905, the Wyanokies were abandoned to nature. Soon after, the first trails were cut. In one of history's accidents, the coming of the automobile and the rise of hiking
coincided with the demise of the local iron industry. In the 1800s
there was no need for trails; people who wanted or had to walk simply shared the roads with horsemen, wagons, and livestock. By contrast, automobile roads were not so easily shared, and so walkers and
hiking clubs began to cut trails. The Wyanokies were available.

The first trail was constructed in 1913. This was the Post Brook
Trail, in the southern Wyanokies around Chikahokee Falls, which

was blazed by Andrew Scarlett of the Appalachian Mountain Club. Soon after, a pioneer of trail work—Dr. Will S. Monroe—turned his attention to these hills. In the 1920s, aided, as an old edition of the *Walk Book* puts it, "by the oxygenated enthusiasm of fellow members of the Green Mountain Club," Monroe designed and completed most of the other trails in the Wyanokies, including those on today's walk.

A professor at the State Normal School in Montclair, Monroe was one of the creators of the Long Trail in Vermont. Early on he proposed another long trail. This one was to run from the Connecticut River to the Delaware River. The trail was built, but as part of an even longer path; Professor Monroe's trail exists today as the local section of the Appalachian Trail.

As these larger projects took fire, the trails of the Wyanokies gradually became overgrown. Maintenance lagged. In the 1930s the New York/New Jersey Trail Conference was invited by local hiking clubs to do what it was already doing in Harriman Park: oversee the trail system, assign maintainers, and consider proposals for new trails.

Today the Conference works with its member clubs to keep up the trails. For instance, here at the dam, two trails cross. The yellow-blazed Mine Trail that continues down along the outlet stream is currently the responsibility of the Metropolitan Recreation Association. The red-blazed Wyanokie Circular that crosses the dam and heads up the hill to the east is maintained by the Nassau Hiking and Outdoor Club. All the work on these trails, and on the Appalachian Trail in this area, the Long Path to the Catskills, and the rest of the eight hundred miles of trails in the metropolitan area under Conference responsibility, is done by volunteers: people from all walks of life who come out once or twice a year to cut brush, remove fallen trees, and repaint blazes.

The Conference also puts out a walking map of the Wyanokies, and of other favorite walking areas. We publish DAY WALKER and its companion book, the *Walk Book*, which is an encyclopedia of all the trails in the metropolitan area as far away as the Catskills and the Taconics. Our newsletter is the *Trail Walker*, a bimonthly tabloid covering all the local walking news; it is sent free to all members of the Conference. Obviously, if you care about nature and walking, we'd like you to be a member of the Conference (G.P.O. Box 2250, New York, NY 10001), and that's our story.

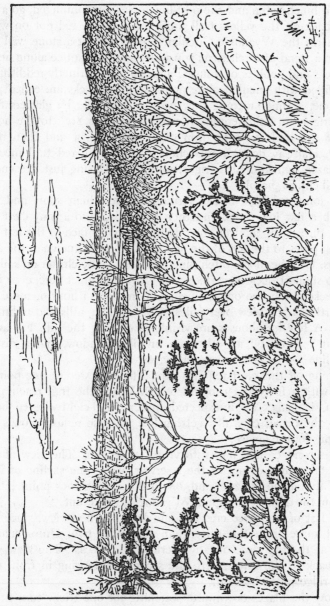

Wanaque Reservoir and New York skyline from Pine Paddy No. 3

With lunch eaten and the post-lunch cleanup completed, go a few paces back on the yellow trail until you find the red dot on white that marks the Wyanokie Circular. Follow it over a stone wall and up into a stand of birches. As you walk, you may notice along here a few rocks and pebbles of unusual appearance—distinctly reddish and often filled with smaller white pebbles. These rocks are called puddingstone, a conglomerate; they were carried here by glaciers from their origins on Schunemunk Mountain in New York to the north.

Now the trail starts to drop off, gently at first and then more steeply. Halfway down a rock-choked ravine, the red trail meets a blue-blazes trail and turns right, joining it. Having just descended, the trail climbs sharply.

The joint red/blue blazes surmount a few high spots and slog through a few low spots, and then they head into a piny cleft. An abrupt turn sends the trail directly up the rocky face to the left and through pines to the top of the first of three crests known as the Pine Paddies. Here hemlock, pitch pine, and white pine cluster on soil too poor to support deciduous trees. It is warm and quiet here; even on a fine weekend day, no one may come along for an hour or more. To the northeast is a view over miles of high rolling hills and unbroken woods. A few farmhouses are visible just below the hill. Far away, sunlight sparkles off an otherwise invisible window, and a distant power line swoops lazily over a valley.

Coming off this crest requires care. The rock step at one point is small, with a forty-foot drop-off below. When the trail reaches the bottom, it makes an unexpected hundred-and-eighty-degree bend. Follow the blazes carefully; getting lost in these remote woods can be serious for the novice.

The second crest comes into view before long. The view at this height takes in a corner of the reservoir below, the skyline of New York City on the horizon, and, off to the right, a rock point jutting out from the ridge—the popular Wyanokie High Point.

The last of the three crests should have the best view, since it is set out more from the ridge than the other two. Unfortunately, woods at the top close off any overlook to the east. The view west looks back to the forest, with the second crest rising in front of a higher ridge on the horizon.

Follow the blazes downward, watching for one tricky turn to the right. An excellent view to the east comes along just before the trail begins its descent into the forest. The skyline of New York is in the distance, with Wyanokie High Point nearly on the right. Much more of the reservoir can be seen from here than from either of the other two crests. The Weis Ecology Center is directly below but hidden from view by the brow of the ridge.

This spot is usually windy; from here, the trail drops down the hillside, passing other, more sheltered viewpoints. The drop to the valley is about three hundred feet in a quarter of a mile, but it is never that steep, and the pool at the bottom comes into view all too quickly. A short walk through the woods and around the pool, crossing the pool's inlet stream, leads out to Snake Den Road, where a left turn shortly brings the trail back to the parking lot.

The Wyanokies are hard to find, but such is the price of remoteness; and the Wyanokies are remote. No bus delivers walkers to the trailhead. The most reasonable form of public transport is the rented car, preferably jammed with hiking friends. The mileage charge will be reasonable—after all, the Wyanokies are only 30 miles from the George Washington Bridge.

—WALT HOUCK and FRANK PERUTZ

25

Paterson and Garret Mountain

Paterson offers the walker a unique opportunity to retrace in a few hours the development of urban America. In this five-mile walk one can experience its still unspoiled natural beauty as well as its industrial growth, decline, and present rebirth.

Paterson is easily reached by bus or car. By bus from New York City, take the Maplewood or Inter City bus No. 30 from the Port Authority Terminal to Market and Church streets, the last stop in Paterson. (This bus runs frequently on a regular schedule.) Traveling by car from the George Washington Bridge involves taking Route 4 west for about fifteen miles to the Passaic River, where it becomes Broadway. Drive down Broadway for about two miles. Just past the railroad overpass, turn left onto Memorial Drive (Loop Road). After three blocks, make a right onto Market Street, and go one block on Market Street to Church Street. Parking is free on Sundays at parking meters. By bus this is a "one-way" walk, whereas by car it is a circular.

The walk begins on the northwest corner of Market and Church streets, the hub of the downtown area, which is now undergoing urban renewal. A six-block walk west along Market Street takes one past the City Hall (an impressive building constructed in 1895 and modeled after the Capitol in Rome, Italy), stately banks, stores, churches, and ethnic neighborhoods.

At Mill Street, the last street before Market makes a jog to the left, turn right and walk three blocks north. At this writing, most of these streets are not marked; use the landmarks for guidance and refer to the maps with this article. While walking up Mill Street, notice an old two-story brick-faced house with gables on the right in the third block. This is the Ryle House, with the three-story Thompson House just to the left. The Ryle House was constructed in the

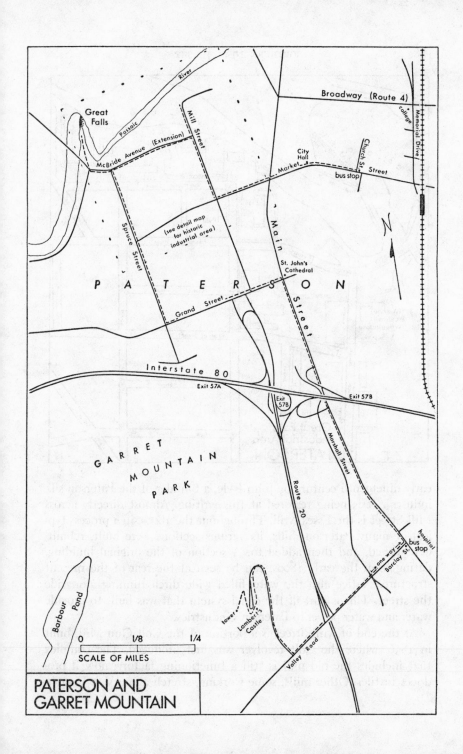

PATERSON AND
GARRET MOUNTAIN

SCALE OF MILES
0   1/8   1/4

Great
Falls

Passaic   River

McBride Avenue (Extension)

Mill Street

Spruce Street

(see detail map
for historic
industrial area)

PATERSON

Broadway (Route 4)

college

Memorial Drive

City Hall

Market   Street

Church St.

bus stop

N

St. John's
Cathedral

Main Street

Grand   Street

Interstate 80

Exit 57A

Exit 57B

Exit 57B

GARRET   MOUNTAIN   PARK

Marshall Street

Route 20

one way

Barclay St.

bus stop

hospital

Barbour Pond

tower

Lambert's
Castle

Valley Road

Great Falls
Industrial Area
PATERSON

early nineteenth century by John Ryle, a founder of the Paterson silk industry. It is being restored at this writing. Almost directly across Mill Street is the Essex Mill. Throughout the 1800s, in a process typical of many Paterson mills, its various sections were built, rebuilt, demolished, and then added to. A section of the original building, dating from the early 1800s, can be seen at the rear of the present structure. Notice also the water-filled wide ditch running alongside the street. This is part of the canal system that was built to provide water and water power to Paterson's industries.

At the end of Mill Street is a portion of the Colt Gun Mill, built in 1836, where the Colt revolver was first produced. The complex that includes the old mill is still a functioning factory; now it produces textiles. Other mills, some working, stretch along Van Houten

Street to the right, with the lily-filled canal in front. These mills, with their tall, thick brick walls and small windows, provide a glimpse into the work environment of the past (and in some cases the present). Double back on Mill Street to the McBride Avenue extension, the first street on the right as you go back toward Market, and turn here up the hill for one long block to an overlook (to the right off Spruce Street and McBride Avenue) of the Great Falls.

The Great Falls of the Passaic River, Paterson, New Jersey

The Great Falls is a breath-taking sight, a natural waterfall that is 77 feet high and 100 feet wide. After heavy rains a rainbow will sometimes form in the gorge over the thundering cascade. In cold weather the spray freezes on the surrounding rocks and vegetation to create a vision of shimmering, crystalline beauty.

Continue along McBride Avenue to a sidewalk that goes off to the right past a low building. This leads to a footbridge that crosses high over the deep chasm at the base of the falls. A small park on the other side of the Passaic River has picnic tables. (Rest rooms are available back at the overlook.) Occasionally, the walker may be lightly sprinkled with spray from the falls, a refreshing experience on a hot day.

During the Revolutionary War, George Washington, Lafayette,

and Alexander Hamilton were encamped in this area and almost surely marveled at the beauty of the falls. After the war, Hamilton returned not for the beauty but for the potential of the falls as a source of power. Under Hamilton's leadership Paterson became the first planned industrial city in the United States.

After lingering awhile at the falls, return to McBride Street and walk back to Spruce Street. Spruce Street is the second street branching off McBride to the right, just before the parking lot for the falls overlook. Continue three blocks south on Spruce. The first and, for a while, only building on the right is the wheelhouse for the Ivanhoe Papermill. Here power was generated for the mill using the water from the canal system. The wheelhouse will eventually be used as the Great Falls Visitor Center. Behind the building is the Middle Raceway, now being restored, that was part of the canal; the system was originally designed by the famous architect Pierre L'Enfant, who also designed the plan for Washington, D.C.

Farther down Spruce Street, at Market Street, is the locomotive complex. The largest building, the one on the left just past Market, once housed the Rogers Company, which produced steam locomotives from 1837 to 1913. At its peak, in 1873, the works could produce one locomotive every second day. Today, two locomotives are exhibited at the entrance; inside are models of machinery, a photographic exhibit of Paterson's industrial history, and the second submarine made by John Holland, the inventor of the submarine. Guided tours of the entire Great Falls Historical District start from here.

Continuing on Spruce to Grand past other mills, turn left and walk four blocks east to Main Street, passing through a neighborhood occupied formerly by the millworkers and presently by Paterson's newest immigrant groups. On the far corner of Main and Grand streets stands St. John's Cathedral. Dedicated in 1870, this imposing brownstone building houses an impressive altar and beautiful stained glass windows; it seats over 1,700 worshipers.

Turn right on Main Street and walk three quarters of a mile south to Barclay Street, again passing through various ethnic neighborhoods. Barclay Street begins opposite St. Joseph's Hospital; turn right and continue to Valley Road across the Route 20 overpass. To the right a turreted castle stands on the crest of a hill: Lambert's Castle. Turn right at the entrance of the Garret Mountain Reserva-

Paterson, path leading to top of escarpment

tion and go up a gentle slope to the castle. This palatial home was
built in 1891 by an immigrant who had become wealthy as a silk
manufacturer. (Paterson was once known as the Silk City of the
United States.) Walk around the castle to its portico entrance,
flanked with stone lions that look out upon a formal green. The
castle now houses the offices of the Passaic County Park Commission
and the Passaic County Historical Museum. The museum is open
Wednesday through Sunday from 1 P.M. to 4 P.M., and the admission
charge is nominal. The rooms are open to the public and have many
paintings and antiques. Note particularly the stained glass windows
and the elaborately decorated ceilings and woodwork, including
scrollwork on the newelposts. One room contains furniture used by
Garret A. Hobart of Paterson, who was Vice-President of the United
States in McKinley's first administration.

After leaving the castle, turn left and go up the steps, then turn
right and follow a switchback trail for a quarter of a mile to the top
and the observation tower. This tower, a tall stone medieval-looking
structure, was used by the castle's original owner as an observatory. It

is not open to the public at this writing, but the trail along the edge of the cliff affords a magnificent panoramic view of the New York City skyline and the entire area.

Return to the castle and walk down the slope to Valley Road, turn left over the Route 20 overpass to Barclay Street, and continue down Barclay Street to Main Street. Bus users can catch the No. 30 bus to the Port Authority Terminal in New York City at this corner. Car travelers will turn left on Main Street and walk one mile to Main and Market streets, turning right on Market Street to Market and Church, the beginning of the walk. Drive north on Church Street to Broadway and turn right. In about two miles Broadway becomes Route 4, which leads to the George Washington Bridge.

—ROSE, MURRAY, and MICHAEL ROSS

Watchung Reservation

One of the finest areas of New Jersey to get lost in is the Watchung Reservation. Paths and old roads head in every direction; the blazing of the trails is erratic; the upper slopes consist of featureless and dense deciduous forest; and most of the available maps are wrong. A noted local trekker, skilled in the navigation of the Adirondack and White Mountains, found himself digging for his seldom-used compass, and then he got lost anyway.

But he didn't stay lost for long. After all, the reservation is in the middle of suburbia, only 30 miles southwest of the George Washington Bridge; no part of its 2,000 acres is far from the many roads that encircle it. The two hillsides and the brook and lake between them run in almost a straight line; and, if geographical clues don't suffice, the park is popular enough that other walkers are almost always passing by.

So, if getting lost under ideal conditions sounds attractive, head for the Watchung Reservation. The walk here is about three miles long, with easy footing.

The hardest part is the first step: finding the reservation, which is a unit of the excellent Union County park system. It is tucked into the hills between Summit, on the north, and Scotch Plains and Mountainside on the south. The drive begins easily enough. Exit the Garden State Parkway at Union onto Route 22 going west. Drive 5.5 miles to the light at New Providence Road (just past a pedestrian overpass) and turn right. Now, in the tangled maze of suburban streets, the fun begins. Signs to the reservation abound, evidently placed to distract the unwary. Drive straight on up the hill on New Providence. Ignore the fact that the name of the street changes mysteriously to Deer Path.

After about three quarters of a mile the road bears left. Take the

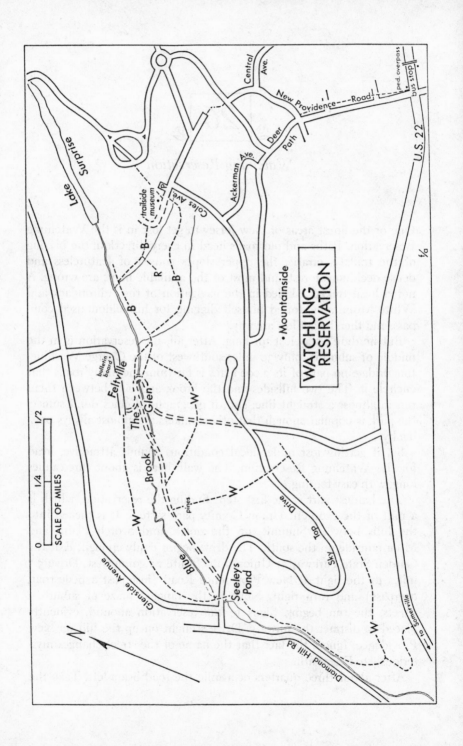

WATCHUNG RESERVATION

SCALE OF MILES

0   1/4   1/2

Lake Surprise

trailside museum

Coles Ave.

Central Ave.

New Providence — Road

ped. overpass

bus stop

Deer Path

Ackerman Ave.

U.S. 22

Mountainside

bulletin board

Feltville

The Glen

Brook

pines

Sky Top Drive

Blue

Glenside Avenue

Seeleys Pond

Diamond Hill Rd

to Somerville

N

second right, which is Ackerman Avenue. This winds up the hill
through a fine residential neighborhood and comes to a T intersection at Coles Avenue. Directly across is unbroken forest—the reservation. Turn here to the right and go to a sharp ninety-degree
bend, where Coles suddenly becomes New Providence Road again.
At this bend, turn left and park in the large parking lot by the
Trailside Museum.

For bus riders, catch the Somerset Bus Lines coach out Route 22
from the Port Authority Terminal. Call (201) 659-8823 for information on departure times. Start looking for New Providence Road
after Route 22 crosses the Garden State Parkway. The two stops before New Providence Road are Summit Road and Central Avenue.
Watch for the pedestrian overpass just before the stop; not only does
it mark New Providence Road but it also leads over to the bus stop
for the return trip.

The bus rider's hike begins at Route 22. The forty-minute stroll up
to the reservation is a good walk in its own right; the climb is two
hundred and fifty feet. From the bus stop, a bike path runs up the
right-hand side of New Providence Road. This pleasant route meanders through the trees and shrubs along the road, often out of sight
of the traffic. White asters grow at the edge of the path, and the
houses and backyards of the neighborhood can be seen through the
trees.

After about half a mile, the bike path comes to a four-way intersection, New Providence Road takes a sharp right here, with Whip-
poorwill the street opposite. Note this again: the street that was New
Providence continues straight ahead, becoming Deer Path; New
Providence Road makes a sharp right. Follow New Providence; unfortunately, there's no sidewalk.

After a quarter of a mile, New Providence turns up the hill, with
Central Avenue continuing straight ahead and then down. Now
heading directly up the hill, with woods on both sides, New Providence comes to an apparent "T" intersection. This is Ayers Drive,
which enters the reservation, but not where the trails start.

Continue straight across the street. There you will find a rutted
dirt road winding around the hill to the right and up. At the top of
the hill this meets the end of a dead-end street: New Providence
Road. Straight ahead on the road brings you to the intersection with
Coles Avenue, the parking lot, the Trailside Museum, and the start
of the trails.

The Trailside Museum is the rambling brown wood structure a little down the hill from the parking lot. At the museum are natural history exhibits, maps, and rest rooms. It's open from noon to 6 P.M. on weekends.

Across the park road from the museum is the trailhead. It is a log archway with an overhead sign reading, "Nature Trail." Go directly down the hillside here to a bridge that crosses a rocky stream. The man-made world is soon left behind. On the other side of the brook the trail bears right through pleasant if nondescript woods. Notice the blazing. Dabs of paint represent the route of the various trails that fan out from the museum. The trails of this walk include the blue blaze of the Copper Mine Trail and the white X of the Sierra Trail. But the woodland corridor is also splashed with green and orange blazes, marking short trails for youngsters. The visual effect of all these blazes in a small area is rather remarkable.

Before long a sturdy bridge can be seen on the right, carrying a bridle trail across a branch of Blue Brook. Soon after, the trails join the bridle trail, which is little used. The white X now departs left, while the Copper Mine Trail continues with the blue blaze through a level wood. It becomes increasingly apparent, however, that the blue trail will not remain level: the drop-off to the left, which has been in view, is now matched by a similar drop-off to the right, and both are edging nearer the trail. The old copper mine is now nearby, but the traces cannot be spotted except by local experts.

Finally the deciduous forest begins to give way to conifers—mostly eastern hemlocks—and through the foliage to the left one can see, at first dimly and then more clearly, the scenery that makes the Watchungs so special. The hillside across the gully is *steep*, dizzyingly so, and heavily wooded.

Although the highest point in the reservation is less than six hundred feet, it all feels much higher. The Watchungs are volcanic in origin, like the Palisades. But, unlike the Palisades, where the molten rock formed a layer underground that was subsequently uncovered by erosion, the Watchungs are a result of surface flows which created a double ridge of mountains that passes in an arc all the way through central New Jersey from Suffern in the north almost to Somerville in the south.

The two drop-offs come together, and the trail begins to descend, as the white blazes rejoin from the left. The path abruptly arrives at the bottom of the slope, a confusing spot where the blue blazes turn away to the right and unmarked trails scatter in all directions. Follow the white blaze ahead and through a muddy patch. Soon you come to a well-defined unmarked trail that slants off to the right, as the Sierra Trail continues up the hill.

This unmarked trail leads out onto a low, porchlike rocky point, with Blue Brook just below. Descend and find a rocky shallow ford, with the ruins of a man-made wall just on the other side of the brook. Cross here. (If the water is too high, go back to the Sierra Trail and continue up until you reach a road. Follow the road down; it will cross the brook on the bridge below Feltville.)

Once across the stream, continue downstream, down the hill from what looks like an old road but is actually the ruins of a millrace canal. The unmarked path soon reaches an intersection where a road comes across the brook and curves up the hill. Another road continues ahead, along the brook.

This whole area is known as the Glen; wild and scenic now, it was once a community of two hundred people. The main part of the settlement is at the top of the hill to the right, up the road. If you're taking the long walk described below, there's no need to see the village now, because that trail will return through the village. But if you are on the short walk, you might want to go up and have a look around.

The village, known as Feltville in its heyday, was founded around 1845 by David Felt, a New York merchant. On the hill are two rows of old houses. Once the workers at the paper mill lived here. Now these buildings are classrooms, where short courses in nature study are taught to groups from the Union County schools. The grounds of Felt's mansion are down the road to the right. Past a bend in the road are the former school and church/general store of the settlement. At the turn itself is a bulletin board with pictures and a text that tells the story of Feltville.

Turn back down to the Glen. As you come down the road, notice the large foundations next to the road that follows Blue Brook. This was the paper mill, and it was still standing at the turn of the century.

Felt departed in the 1860s and took the secret of prosperity with him. Now, as you stand by the river, the sunlight filters down through the tall conifers. The stream is so clear that the rocks on the bottom can be counted like stars in the sky. The hillside is steep and shadowed and the foliage is dense; it's difficult not to be reminded of the Adirondacks. Perhaps most remarkable is the quiet. There are other spots in the metropolitan area that *look* primeval, but few that fool the ear as well. Here, the ridges deflect the usually inescapable urban hum.

Eventually the walk continues downstream along the road. The ravine bottom now opens up somewhat, with high trees and tall weeds. The road forks, with the right fork running up the hill and turning into a trail. Stay left, past a clump of spotted touch-me-nots.

By now the drama of the Glen is behind, and Blue Brook is meandering in a meadow. A little after the road crosses the stream, maybe a third of a mile past the Glen, the white blaze once again comes in from the left. Here a decision must be made.

One choice is to take the long walk, continuing ahead on the road. The Sierra Trail turns off the road after a while and climbs to the top of the eastern ridge through a pine plantation. It continues to the southern edge of the reservation, with dramatic views across the valley to a quarry. Swinging northwest, it cuts behind Seeleys Pond and follows the western ridge back to Feltville. It continues along the ridge and around Lake Surprise and circles through the north end of the reservation. Since numerous trails and woods roads go from the ridgetops to the valleys, walks of ten and more miles can be easily fashioned.

This walk, however, chooses a less strenuous alternative. Turn away from the road, following the white blaze left and up the hill. The trail makes a long and gradual ascent along an eroded old road through a hardwood forest. Close to the top an unmarked trail diverges to the right and out of the reservation. In about half a mile from the road, just after reaching the top, the trail crosses a small but perennial brook—one interesting fact about the reservation is that so many of the brooks, although small, continue flowing even in late summer and fall.

Just beyond the brook, an old dirt road crosses, with houses visible to the right; this is Glenside Road, which goes down to the Glen and crosses Blue Brook on the bridge there. Hemlocks now begin to appear and then the trail turns away from the trees and heads back down into the ravine.

As before, the hemlocks signal the beginning of another abrupt

Watchung Reservation, Lake Surprise

gully. Attention to the blazes is needed here. The white-blazed Sierra Trail drops steeply left. At the bottom it crosses the stream and goes up to the right, then zigzags down to the Glen, where earlier you took the unmarked trail across Blue Brook to the millrace ruins. Retrace your steps past the muddy spot to the bottom of the drop-off where the blue trail turned away, and then follow the blue trail along the brook.

Notice that soon after you get on it the blue trail forks, with both forks marked in blue. One fork runs along the base of the hill and the other a little up the slope, parallel to the lower trail and maybe twenty feet above it. The reason for this paradoxical layout is apparent after a rain: the lower trail tends to get waterlogged, so park officials provided an alternative.

Soon after the two trails rejoin, they fork again. Where they rejoin a second time, an unmarked trail goes ahead along Blue Brook, heading for Lake Surprise. The blue blazes, which we are following here, cross a bridge and then head up along a side stream.

After a red-blazed trail joins from the right, the blue blazes curve away from the stream and up a rock-strewn draw, turning left just before reaching a large grass meadow with an old green barn off to the left. Follow the gravel road that leads to the right, out of the meadow and past the Trailside Museum to the start of the walk.

The Watchung Reservation has many other activities. Nature, scientific, and astronomical shows are put on at the science center, which is the modern building a short distance west of the parking lot. Beyond the center, on the other side of the trees, is a large playing field with a refreshment stand that is open in season. Horses can be rented from stables located at the far north end of the park. Cross-country ski workshops are conducted in the winter.

Many walkers hike the reservation in spring, when the flowering dogwood and rhododendron are at their peak bloom. Try going instead in the winter. When so many local areas look stark and bare, the hemlocks of the Glen will still be verdant, tranquil, and timeless.

—WALT HOUCK and BILL HOLZSCHUH, JR.

CENTRAL NEW JERSEY:
The View From Here

The countryside north and west of the metropolitan area is rich in contrast—the vast yellowing columns of the Palisades, the lofty gray ledges of the Ramapos, the boulders of Blue Mountain, the hemlock-choked gorges of the Watchungs, the rugged shoreline of Pelham Bay Park.

To move south into central New Jersey is to leave all this behind. The topography here is flat, a coastal plain sloping gently to the sea. This is a countryside of estuaries, fields, low hills, and slow-flowing streams. Typical are Cheesequake State Park and the Delaware and Raritan Canal—Cheesequake, where sandy roads skirt marshes that teem with life; the canal, gliding peacefully past farms and villages. Compared to the rock ledges and tumbling brooks of the north, this is a different texture of life: more leisurely, less demanding, simply less *hard*.

Many walkers will never visit these unspectacular points south. Others will seek them out, with DAY WALKER or *Walk Book* in hand, because for them diversity is one of the great pleasures of the life afoot.

The spectacular will always gain our attention; but diversity is what holds it in the long run. The teenagers shoulder their backpacks, on their way to Harriman Park or the more distant Catskills or Adirondacks. The young adult turns lightweight strider, burning up the miles on the Croton Aqueduct, with every muscle glowing in rhythmic harmony. The parent watches the youngster frolic on a sunny path in Muttontown Preserve. One person goes forth to explore; another returns a hundred times to a single special corner—a holly forest on Fire Island, a piney knoll in the Wyanokies. Over a lifetime of walking, the metropolitan walker can be every one of these people.

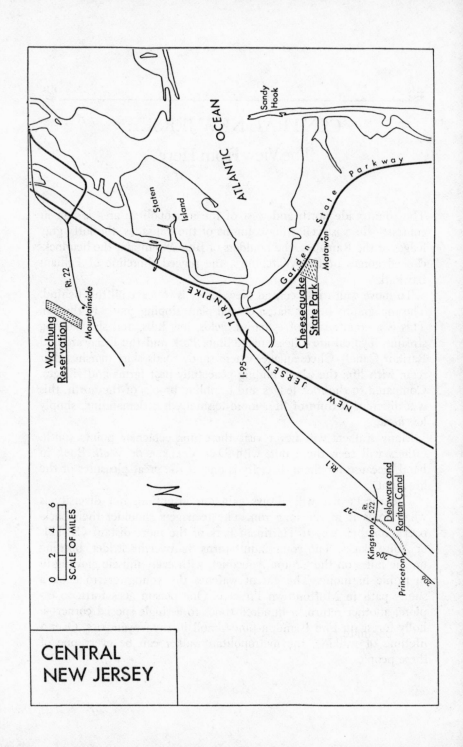

CENTRAL
NEW JERSEY

SCALE OF MILES

0   2   4   6

N

ATLANTIC OCEAN

Sandy
Hook

Garden State Parkway

Matawan

Cheesequake
State Park

TURNPIKE

NEW JERSEY

I-95

Rt. 22

Mountainside

Watchung
Reservation

Staten
Island

Rt. 1

Kingston

Rt.
522

Princeton

27

206

206

518

Delaware and
Raritan Canal

Cheesequake State Park

Cheesequake State Park lies just inland from the northernmost end of the New Jersey shore and just south of the industrial belt that stretches through Newark, Elizabeth, and the Amboys, some 40 miles south of the George Washington Bridge. Within a relatively small area, Cheesequake contains many habitats—the predominant sandy-soil upland woods; a meadow full of wildflowers, and, in the lowlands, salt-water and fresh-water marshes and a cedar swamp. Borderlines between habitats are abrupt, often surprisingly so.

This two-hour walk winds through woodlands and fresh-water swamp areas. It offers occasional glimpses of the salt marsh that extends from the north and west corners of the park. This marsh is one of a string of salt marshes which lie along the Jersey coast and indeed along the whole eastern seaboard—the most notable (or notorious) in this area being the Hackensack Meadows.

In spite of the fact that the marsh covers relatively little of the area of the park, it contributes much to the park's quality—Hook's Creek Lake, the unique plants and wildlife, the peaceful and solitary atmosphere of the grasslands. Salt marshes—as distinct from fresh-water marshes—occur when low-lying land is periodically flooded by tidal creeks (in this case, a network of creeks, including Cheesequake Creek and Hook's Creek), which vary the salinity of their brackish water according to whether the tide is high or low. The plants we are familiar with from woodland hikes could not exist in such a habitat because they could not tolerate either the amount of salt or the variation in salt content in the water. Therefore, the plants and animals which populate the salt marsh are specially adapted to this environment. Naturalist Tom Braden suggests that a visitor to Cheesequake may expect to find blue herons, snowy egrets, muskrat, turtles, and diamond-backed terrapin around the marsh, and plentiful fish in

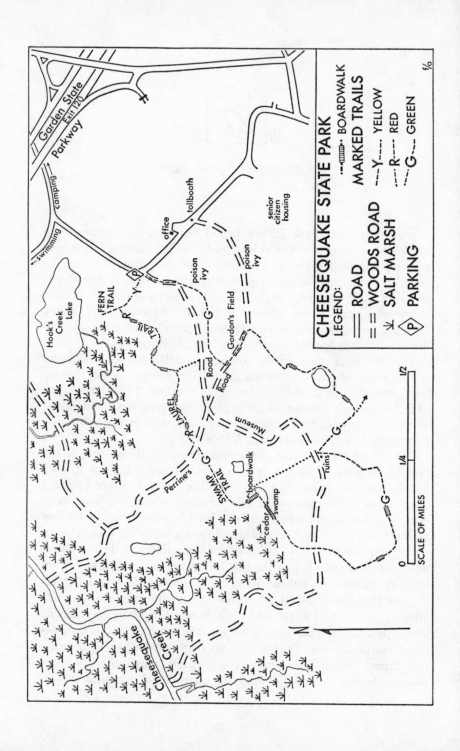

CHEESEQUAKE STATE PARK

LEGEND:

MARKED TRAILS
- BOARDWALK
- Y — YELLOW
- R - - - RED
- G · · · GREEN

ROAD
WOODS ROAD
SALT MARSH
PARKING

Garden State Parkway   Exit 120

swimming
camping

Hook's Creek Lake

office
tollbooth

senior citizen housing

FERN TRAIL

poison ivy
poison ivy

Gordon's Field

Road
Road

R LAUREL TRAIL

Museum

Perrine's

SWAMP TRAIL G

boardwalk
cedar swamp

ruins   G

G

Cheesequake Creek

N

SCALE OF MILES
0   1/4   1/2

Hook's Creek Lake. Oysters, clams, and crab live in the marsh, and many kinds of commercially important fish spend part of their lives in the tidal waters.

The dominant plant which you will see as you look out over the marsh is *Spartina,* a fine grass once harvested for salt hay, a farm animal food. From colonial times to the nineteenth century, farms near the seashore were particularly prized if they contained salt marsh acreage. In some Jersey shore areas where the marsh was fairly firm, cattle actually grazed on the marsh, except during the green-headed fly season, when the insects were so distracting that the cattle could not eat. Unless you wade out into the marsh, however (and this is *not* something to do unless you are thoroughly familiar with the area, since mud under a salt marsh may be fifteen or more feet deep), you probably won't be able to see *Spartina* close up. Rather, you'll see *Phragmites,* a tall (perhaps seven feet) reed with an arched, feathery head, which grows along the edge of the marsh. It is not native to the United States but has spread rapidly since being introduced, and can be found in almost any wet patch along a highway. You'll also see many other grasses whose dried heads and stalks are beautiful even on a winter hike.

Salt marshes have traditionally been particularly maligned and mistreated: they have been dyked, drained, filled, used as garbage dumps. Having myself grown up near the Hackensack Meadows, and been repelled by the unpleasant smells and ugly, blighted landscapes broken by an occasional radio transmitter, I was deeply moved by the slightly tangy salt air of the marsh and the relatively undisturbed, shimmering expanses of golden-shaded *Spartina.* My nine-year-old daughter was enchanted by the marsh's stillness and by the many beautiful grasses which grow at its edge. A not always willing hiker, she walked without protest the extra mile to explore the marsh from several approaches.

If you'd like to get more of a feel for the salt marsh, you can take a detour in the hike described below by turning right onto Museum Road, after you've passed through the cedar swamp. Follow the road out past a gate, take the right branch of the road, and follow it until it dead-ends at Cheesequake Creek in the midst of the marsh. Or you can walk out on Perrine's Road and take marked paths either to Cheesequake Creek or across Hook's Creek to Hook's Creek Lake. (If you are interested in reading more about salt marshes, I strongly recommend John and Mildred Teal's *Life and Death of the Salt Marsh*, published in 1972 by Audubon/Ballantine in paperback.)

Cheesequake's former farmlands were made into a park during the 1930s by the WPA. However, the trail system is quite new, the first paths having been cleared in 1977 with the aid of the Youth Conservation Corps (YCC). A naturalist joined the summer staff in 1978 and developed a self-guiding booklet for a short trail around Hook's Creek Lake. Superintendent Bill Vibbert plans to extend hiking trails and nature study programs to new areas of the park, and he has already modified one of the existing trails. Hikers should check with the park office for the most up-to-date trail information.

The trails are, almost without exception, very easy to follow and exceptionally well blazed. Blazes are colored circles and arrows on wooden plaques attached to trees. Each trail system is coded a different color. There are also a number of unmarked paths, fine for exploring. As one would expect in a marsh area, some of the park trails are quite muddy, no matter what the season; both insect repellent and appropriate footwear are strongly advised. And that attractive ground cover which grows along the sides of sand roads and over some of the old horse trails is likely to be poison ivy—beware! Some particularly lush sites are indicated on the map.

The hike described here is a loop. There are a number of points along the way at which you can turn back to the start, making hikes of varying lengths. The entire hike, start to finish, is three to three and a half miles long and should take an average walker one and a half to two hours, not counting time for lunch, rests, photographs, and exploring.

Start from the nature trails parking area, on the left shortly past the park entrance and just beyond the office. There is a wooden trail map there and signposts for the Fern, Laurel and Cedar Swamp trails—all loops. All trails begin together. Soon after the start, the trails fork. Follow the left-hand trail, which goes slightly downhill and is blazed red and yellow. In a short while you will come to another fork. Straight ahead is the Fern Trail, blazed yellow. A self-guided nature trail booklet is available at the office for this trail. Our hike, following a sign and red arrow, turns left onto the Laurel Trail. In the spring huge stands of fiddleheads and skunk cabbage are found at this turn. Cross the first of many boardwalk-type bridges and climb uphill, noting the high-bush blueberries, whose white bell-shaped flowers bloom in May. Loop back and downhill (watch out for the mud) to an overview of the salt marsh, ringed with *Phragmites*. This view, which is very impressive in winter and spring, is not visible during the height of summer growth. Here the trail appears to turn left and right: go left, continuing downhill, through more mud, to the second bridge. The third bridge follows immediately. Cross it and climb up a steep little rise. Just after the top, the trail bears left. Soon another path intersects the trail from the left; there may or may not be a log barring it. This side path leads to a road which returns, left, to the parking lot.

Continuing on the main trail, note the shrubs along the edges. The most frequent, appearing not just on this trail but in many low-lying areas throughout the park, are called *Clethra*, or sweet pepper bush. They have alternate, toothed, thin oval leaves and both gray and brown bark. I first noticed them in late August, when their spikes of small white five-petaled flowers filled the air with a delicious lilac-like scent.

After walking for a few minutes you will come to three more bridges, which are really walkways over muddy places. Notice the tree whose trunk is bent like the handle of a brace and bit, just before you come to a sand road—Perrine's Road. The red arrow indicates a left turn to complete the Laurel Trail loop. This makes a thirty-minute hike if you turn back here to the parking lot. (Returning by the road, you will come to a four-cornered intersection. Take the road to your left.) To continue the hike, cross the road and enter the woods at the sign for the Cedar Swamp Trail, blazed green. In a few minutes you'll come to the top of a ridge. Just before the top, look closely at the bases of trees on your right. If you're lucky, you may find a cluster of chanterelle mushrooms in delicate hues of creamy orange.

At the top of the ridge, the trail forks. A faint path goes off to the right, leading down into the marshlands for exploring. The main trail goes straight ahead downhill, skirting a beautiful stand of *Phragmites*. In late fall to spring you can walk right down into the reeds, which will be higher than your head. A faint trail continues along the edge of the marsh, and I have seen red fox here. Following the green arrow, the main trail goes left, up a very steep rise, then down the other side to a boardwalk over a fresh-water marsh. In August and September this area is overflowing with wildflowers: pink and white smartweed; purplish joe-pye weed and monkey flowers shaped like a monkey's face; fuzzy white water horehound; and the orange stems and white flowers of parasitic dodder growing on orange-spotted touch-me-not. If you should happen to wander into any of the lush poison ivy growing in Cheesequake, the juice from the stem of touch-me-not, or jewelweed, will relieve the itching. There are benches at the far end of the boardwalk for rest, lunch, or just enjoying.

On the other side of the fresh-water marsh, the trail again forks. Should you wish to end your hike here, turn left and, at the four-

Cheesequake Park, cypress swamp boardwalk

cornered intersection, go straight ahead, returning to the parking area. Otherwise, to continue, take the right fork; a moment later, the trail divides again. Follow the green arrow and take the right fork, which leads down some steps onto a boardwalk winding most pleasantly through a corner of a tiny cedar swamp, a dark, wet area with beautiful lacy cedars looming overhead. When I first hiked in this area there was no boardwalk and, in all but the driest season, the trail was at best extremely muddy and, at worst, impossible to find. It's lovely now. Returning to primarily deciduous woods, you will arrive at Museum Road in about ten minutes of walking. (Remember, if you want to visit the salt marsh, make a right turn here.) Enter the woods again on the other side of the road, still following the green blazes. Along the trail are several large white pines, with their fluffy-looking, five-needle clusters. A park staff person reported many hawk sightings in this area. After three or four minutes of gentle climbing, turn left, following the green arrow, and cross a stepped bridge over the eroded mud. Just past the top of the rise, follow the green arrow and turn left again. Here in late August and early September your nose will alert you that sweet pepper bush is nearby. After a few minutes the trail follows an S-curve to cross a bridge. There are benches here in a lovely setting, but the traffic noise from a nearby highway may be discouraging.

On the other side of the bridge, go down an incline and up the "steps" on the other side. At the top the trail splits, one branch going off to the right and the other going left. Follow the latter, as the arrow indicates. A moment later, follow the green arrow as the trail turns right around a small series of sandy clearings on your left, then crosses a bridge. Follow the markers as the trail winds through small groves of pine trees, their evergreen needles particularly lovely against the stark buff sand. Watch for a left turn in the trail, and when you've made it, note an enormous patch of ground pine to the left of the path. Its resemblance to miniature Christmas trees and resulting wholesale use in Christmas decorations has made this an endangered species—so look, but do not pick. A little farther on, mountain laurel borders the trail, surrounding it in early June with puffs of pink to white blossoms. After three to four minutes you will come to a fork, in the middle of which are the ruined foundations of a building. The left path leads to a deserted parking lot. Take the right fork past the ruins of the old museum, for which Museum

Road is named. According to Park Superintendent Vibbert, the museum was built in the late 1930s, never used, and was destroyed in the early 1950s.

At the next split in the trail you can either return to the parking lot via the left fork to Museum Road, for a total hike of approximately seventy-five minutes, or you can take the right fork and extend your hike another thirty to forty-five minutes. The right fork leads onto a portion of the old horse trail, blazed green.

This section of trail is interesting because part of it runs along the edge of a fresh-water marsh which you can explore if water conditions are favorable. The walk is particularly recommended in late August and early September, when vast expanses of golden tickseed sunflowers bloom in the marsh among the skeletons of dead trees. Be careful walking on the sandy mud at the beginning of the trail—it is extremely slippery. Follow the green blazes back into the woods. After about five minutes the trail splits—right and sharp left. Take the latter. On the right of the trail another sea of sunflowers is visible through an opening in the trees. Cross a bridge, then follow blazes past more mountain laurel. Follow the green arrow when the trail turns right. Straight ahead of you, at the turn, is a stand of Japanese knotweed. This plant, with its hollow, bamboo-like stems and spade-shaped leaves, appears to be a tall shrub but is really an herb which dies back to the ground each year. Its drooping sprays of white flowers in late August and early September readily distinguish it. Japanese knotweed is fairly common in the park.

Soon the trail begins to skirt a fresh-water marsh to the left, full of ghostly dead trees standing in a pool of cloudy water. The trees were killed years ago by chemical dumping, now halted, outside the park which settled into this low area. Vegetation is growing once again, and the contrast between the stark tree trunks and the grasses and vibrant flowers is quite startling. A fellow hiker surprised mallards here. Explore the marsh, if you like and if water conditions permit, noting especially the many beautiful grasses. Then follow the trail around the marsh. Cross a bridge over a stream with a sandy channel that may be bright orange, depending on water conditions, and follow the trail which curves around to the left.

As you go uphill, the trail re-enters the woods. After five to seven minutes, it comes out on a road. Green arrows indicate a left turn. After you've turned, on your right is a large meadow, full of wildflowers. This is Gordon's Field, formerly an Indian campground. Arrowheads found here are on display in the park office. The park allows group camping here. Walk along the road about three hundred feet, watching on the right for a tree with a green arrow and a faint white painted horseshoe. Turn right here, skirting the field. Where the trail seems to head into the meadow, turn left away from the meadow between two birch trees. There is no marker at the turn, but once you have successfully made it, you will see a red and green blaze a short distance away. You will also be able to see Perrine's Road off to the left. Follow a trail around the edge of the meadow, past greenbrier vines on the left. At various points the trail opens into Gordon's Field, which, on this side, is covered in early May by the single fragile flowers of purple lobelia, their slender stems almost invisible against the finely pebbled buff sand. Be careful stepping into the meadow—some of the vegetation growing there is very delicate.

When the trail moves away from the field and toward the road, and goes up, over, and down an incline, turn left to join the road. The return is indicated by a marker. Turn right on the road and return to the parking area in less than five minutes.

Cheesequake offers other recreational opportunities besides hiking, including lifeguard-supervised swimming, family and group camping, and a picnic area. These facilities are much more heavily used than the farther reaches of the hiking trails. A naturalist is on duty on Saturdays between Memorial Day and Labor Day to answer questions and give an evening slide show in the campground; guided hikes can be arranged. From Memorial Day to Labor Day, an admission fee is charged, with an additional fee for camping. Out of season, the park is open and there is no fee except for campers. These fees should be kept in mind when planning a visit, since a trip to Cheesequake on a midsummer weekend along toll roads can be an expensive proposition.

There are several ways to get to Cheesequake. I wasn't able to find any reasonable public transportation, but a fellow hiker has told me that the relatively low cab fare from the Matawan station on the North Jersey Coast Line makes the railroad a possibility.

The usually recommended route by car is the New Jersey Turnpike to the Garden State Parkway. However, tolls are high, and air and scenic quality is poor.

I prefer taking U.S. 1 and 9 south, which doesn't take any longer than the turnpike. Around Newark Airport, stay left to avoid confusing entrances and exits. After this, there are sections of highway which have traffic lights. At Woodbridge, Routes 1 and 9 divide—stay left for 9 south. Shortly after that you will see signs for the Garden State Parkway *and* the New Jersey Turnpike. This exit is for the Parkway *north only*—do not take it. Take the next exit off 9 (left lane), which leads to the Garden State Parkway south. You will stay on the parkway for only a few miles.

After the Raritan toll plaza, the parkway divides into express and local lanes. Be sure to stay right for the local "all exits" lane, and leave the parkway at Exit 120, the second exit after the toll plaza. Very clear signs direct one to the park; but just in case you miss them, follow the exit road to an intersection and turn right. Turn right again at the first traffic light, and then right again at the first stop sign. This road will lead you past a housing development directly into the park. Trails begin on the left not far past the entrance station. Time for the trip is about an hour and ten minutes from Holland Tunnel.

As my hiking companion—a photographer—once remarked, at Cheesequake you use a macro rather than a wide-angle lens. Because of the charming up-and-down folds of the woodland, panoramas are few; when they do exist, they may be marred by distant commercial buildings out in the midst of the salt marsh. The expansive silence of the woods sometimes loses out to traffic noise from nearby Route 34. The sandy woodland foliage is not nearly as dense and lushly green as those of us might expect who are used to walking in Westchester or New England. Instead, the beauty of Cheesequake is most often small and discrete—an ornamental grass head silhouetted against the sky, a few lady's slippers along an old service road, a red fox streaking away, a ray of light filtered through cedar branches, a single blue-gray muscular trunk of an American hornbeam tree.

—JUDY BURNS

The Delaware and Raritan Canal

A five-mile stroll on the towpath of the Delaware and Raritan Canal from Kingston through Princeton will take you back to the past. In the eighteenth century there were marches and battles; in the nineteenth there were barges and barrels. Today the D & R Canal State Park is a flat ribbon of green 55 miles south of the George Washington Bridge, a favored destination for the walker, runner, bicyclist, and canoeist.

Opened in 1834, the canal was a heavy transportation route between Pennsylvania and New York; it replaced the long descent of Delaware Bay and the exposed run up the Jersey coast. The canal ran forty-four miles from Bordentown on the Delaware River through Trenton to New Brunswick at the southern edge of New York Harbor. A thirteen-mile feeder canal brought water from Raven Rock, upriver from Trenton, to provide the current for the canal.

Once the barges were pulled by mules along this towpath. Later, steam-powered tugs provided the power; the locks and bridges were also operated by machine rather than muscle. A few of the buildings constructed to service the canal are still standing.

When the Reading and later the Pennsylvania railroads were built, the canal was doomed, and it gradually fell into disuse. Today, however, the canal is once again important, for it supplies water to almost a million people. The locks and bridges have been rebuilt with concrete and steel, and canoes instead of barges ply the placid water.

Access to the towpath at Kingston is easy. Suburban Transit buses leave New York City every half hour every day of the year and reach Kingston in about an hour and a half. They return from Princeton on the same schedule. Near the bus stop in Kingston are several at-

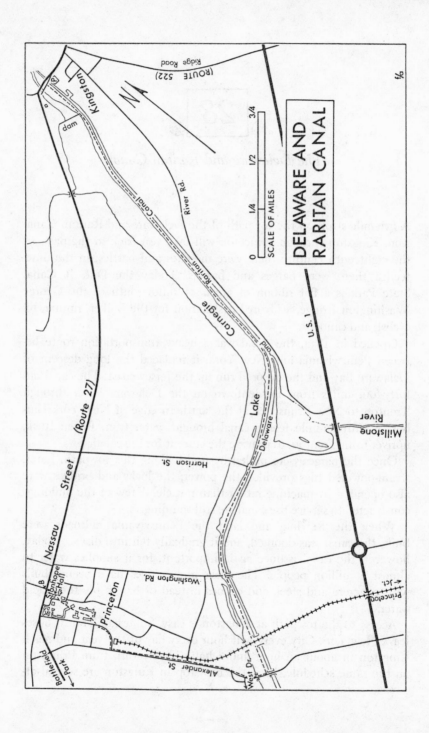

DELAWARE AND
RARITAN CANAL

SCALE OF MILES

0   1/4   1/2   3/4

N

(ROUTE 522)
Ridge Road

Kingston

dam

Canal

River Rd.

Raritan

Carnegie

Lake

and

Delaware

U.S. 1

Millstone
River

Harrison St.

Street

(Route 27)

Nassau

Princeton

Washington Rd.

Princeton
Jct.

Battlefield
Park

Alexander St.

West Dr.

Stanhope
Hall

tractive restaurants. Two blocks farther on (ask the driver to stop at River Road), you can get off the bus right at the park.

Drivers from the metropolitan area should go south on Route 1 to the Kingston turnoff on Ridge Road (Route 522). Turn right at the T intersection and proceed into town, turning left on Route 27. At the foot of the hill is the park, with a parking lot between the canal and the river. From here you can walk to Princeton and take the bus back, or walk as far as you want and then retrace your steps back to the car. [Long-distance walkers can go north from this point fifteen miles to Bound Brook, which is served by the Somerset Bus Lines.— Ed.]

The new Route 27 sweeps north of the parking lot. Old Route 27 angles to the left, crosses a railroad track and a bridge over the canal, and then continues past the entrance to the parking lot. Stop for a moment on the canal bridge. Directly before you is the first of seven locks that let barges down to sea level in New Brunswick (which is behind you, beyond the new highway). The old lock gates have been replaced by the triple sluice gates used today to control the water level. The larger of the white buildings bordering the towpath was formerly the lockkeeper's house. Built in 1832, it is now leased to the operator of a canoe rental service. The smaller white building, now the canoe rental office, is the only surviving telegraph and toll station on the canal. The Morse system was used along the canal and was one of the earliest commercial applications of the then new method of communication.

Canoeists and would-be canoeists will find easy paddling on Lake Carnegie, to the south. Use the canal to return; keep in mind that the canal flows north. Because canoeing here is popular, reservations are advised for weekends. The phone number to call at this writing is (609) 924-9418. Fishing bait can be purchased at the canoe rental office. The canal is stocked by the state, and it is possible to catch bass, trout, and bluegills.

Continue along the old road past the parking area and a pleasant picnic spot under tall trees to the stone bridge over the Millstone River. To your left is the Mill Pond, and upstream is the Lake Carnegie dam. The red building on the right in front of you (not open to the public) is a gristmill built in 1755 by Jacob Skillman.

The stone bridge here was in use from 1798 to about 1968. It replaced an earlier wooden bridge, built in 1700, which was destroyed

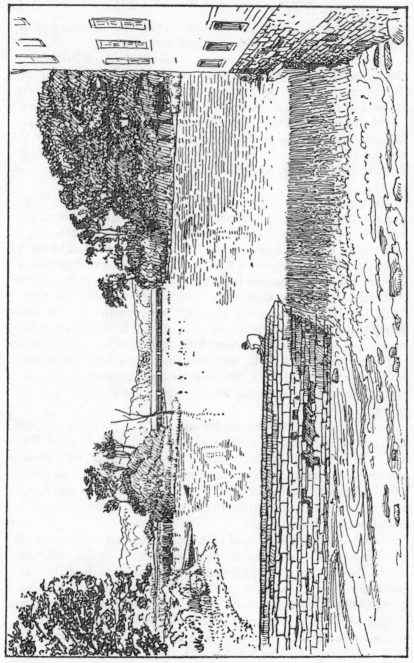

Old mill, Delaware and Raritan Canal, Lake Carnegie in background. After photo by Albert Field

in 1777 by retreating American troops after the Battle of Princeton. After this battle, Washington began to lead his small army north, hoping to raid the British supply depot in New Brunswick. However, it was soon apparent that the army was not strong enough for another battle. In Kingston they burned the bridge without crossing it and headed northwest, toward Morristown. The pursuing British were fooled; they concluded that Washington was headed for New Brunswick, thus ensuring Washington's successful getaway.

Now, return to the canal and start south along the bank, between the lock and the lockkeeper's house. You will see the deep grooves in the top of the rocks where one set of lock gates used to stand. At the far end of the lock are the modern sluice gates. Not long after, the remains of a barge turning basin can be seen on the far side of the canal. A little farther, on the edge of the towpath, are sluice gates to let excess water out of the canal. Where trees start to shade the path, you will cross a slightly lower area covered with stones, an overflow point for minor fluctuations in water level—normally six feet in depth.

Lake Carnegie soon comes into view on the right, with the dam a short distance from the path. The lake was created in 1906 as a gift from steel tycoon Andrew Carnegie to Princeton University. Except during collegiate boating races, it is open to the public. The small concrete structure here is a gauging station of the U. S. Coast and Geodetic Survey.

The delightfully shaded towpath continues between the lake and the canal. At intervals along the right are signs that mark the distances for boat races. The first one, with an "F" on the lake side, is the finish line. Across the lake can be seen the viewing stands and fields.

Route 27, which up to now has been visible across the lake, moves away as the lake makes a gentle bend to the left. Backyards and boathouses of some residences along the highway can be seen. In the opposite direction, across the canal, the bank is fringed with trees and shrubs; a road nears the bank a little farther on.

The milepost on the right tells us we are twenty-six miles from New Brunswick and eighteen from Trenton.

Soon after the lake and canal make a large sweeping bend to the right, the canal crosses the Millstone River where it enters the lake. The crossing is a large concrete aqueduct. The aqueduct is bordered by a seventy-five-yard-long footbridge about five feet wide, with no railing. To the left, across the large pond of the river, Route 1 can be seen, and River Road turns toward it from the canal. The river here is popular with fishermen, who are sometimes successful at outwitting the local bass and sunfish.

Harrison Street crosses the canal and lake three miles from Kingston, providing a short cut to Route 27 about a mile from downtown Princeton. The towpath continues through a grassy park, with the lake no longer to the immediate right. The occasional old willows that grow here were started from twigs brought from a tree near the first burial place of Napoleon on St. Helena Island.

About a mile from Harrison Street, Washington Road bridges the lake. It goes into the center of Princeton past the white-domed gymnasium. The building across the lake just south of the bridge is the boathouse.

Where Stony Brook flows into the end of the lake, the canal passes through a grove of old trees. Shortly beyond is the bridge overhead that carries the railroad into Princeton. This is a short spur line from the main line at Princeton Junction. When the canal was still in operation, the bridge section over the canal and towpath would swing aside to let the tugs pass. Today the rails are continuous and the turning mechanism is gone, but the large gearwheel can be seen atop the central stone pillar, its south side mantled in honeysuckle and poison ivy.

Milepost 28/16 is just beyond, and then Alexander Street. This last section passes the remains of a canal basin. Once there were two basins here, one on either side of Alexander Street. These basins gave the barges a place to tie up out of the main channel, to turn around, and to stop for the night. Little remains of what once was a thriving community here to serve the boatmen. The dilapidated clapboard building across the canal, now a private house, was once the Railroad Hotel; until 1864, when the tracks were removed to their present location, the Camden and Amboy Railroad ran in front of the hotel.

From this point it is possible to continue walking several miles on toward Trenton, but public transportation is lacking at the far end. Turn right on Alexander Street and cross Stony Brook. The first street to your left is West Drive, which leads in a third of a mile to the entrance of the Princeton Wild Life Refuge. This tract is worth an excursion when the ground is not too wet, particularly when wildflowers are in season.

A half mile up Alexander Street from the canal is Faculty Road, one of the stops on the Mercer Metro Loop bus. Service is less than continuous, and exact fare is required. Another third of a mile along Alexander is University Place (and a market). Turn right at this corner. The Princeton railroad station is ahead. You may want to take the shuttle out to the junction to connect with trains for New York or Trenton; the fare is higher than the bus fare, and service is less frequent.

If taking the bus, continue on the footpath that leads from the upper end of the station past modern dormitories on the right to a quadrangle of university buildings. Continue ahead up the stairs under the clock tower of Blair Hall. Take the diagonal to your right, passing between two buildings and continuing until you are in a large grass quadrangle, with old buildings on three sides and a busy street ahead on the fourth. This quadrangle is known as the Front Campus and is the oldest part of the campus.

The building behind you, with the bronze tigers flanking the front steps, is old Nassau Hall. In 1756, Nassau Hall was the entire College of New Jersey. During the Revolutionary War the building was occupied at various times by British and colonial forces, and for about half of 1783 it was the seat of the Continental Congress.

Free guided tours of the campus start from the Maclean House, which is the last building on the far left of the quadrangle just off Nassau Street (Route 27). The tours are conducted by the Orange Key Society.

A historic site not far from the campus is the Princeton battlefield. Shortly after Washington's great Delaware crossing and Christmas Day victory over the Hessians at Trenton, he crossed the Delaware again and routed the British in a swift skirmish just south of Princeton on January 3, 1777, escaping by way of Kingston. Guidebooks to this and other Princeton features can be purchased at the Maclean House, at the stationery stores along Nassau Street, or at the Historical Society of Princeton at 158 Nassau Street, near Washington Road.

Leaving the campus and quadrangle via FitzRandolph gateway, you will find yourself on Nassau Street, with its shops and restaurants. Palmer Square is to your left and Washington Road to your right. The bus station is just across the street, at the corner of Witherspoon Street, and the stop for the return bus to New York City is right here at the benches.

—ALBERT FIELD

ABOUT THIS BOOK

In presenting DAY WALKER as a companion work to its well-known *New York Walk Book*, the New York/New Jersey Trail Conference hopes to encourage young and old alike to enjoy walking as a hobby and to introduce the many nearby green areas that walkers can visit.

DAY WALKER brings together the favorite local walks of more than twenty members and friends of the Conference. The writers, whose names are signed to their contributions, have a wide range of background and outdoor experience. The youngest writer was still in high school when this book was written; the oldest was nearly eighty. Some are strong and dedicated hikers; others don't consider themselves hikers at all but photographers or bird watchers who happen to walk to where the pictures and the birds are. By occupation, the writers are teachers, students, salesmen, housewives, engineers, editors, accountants, graphic designers. All volunteered their work; the royalties from DAY WALKER go directly to the Conference to help maintain trails and protect their surroundings.

Arlene Coccari and Walter Houck directed the project. Arlene found the writers and hike checkers and worked with them; Walt edited the walks. Both found time to contribute walks of their own, and Walt did much of the unsigned writing as well, with help from Ken Mullen for geological information and from Evi Agiewich on walking with children.

Richard Edes Harrison agreed to provide the original sketches for DAY WALKER. A noted artist and cartographer whose work appears in *The New Yorker* and elsewhere, Harrison has influenced the hiking community through his fervent interest in local parks and preserves.

As cartographer for this book, Roger "Strider" Coco contributed the many maps, with an assist from *fox/art*. A dedicated canoeist and outdoorsman, Coco was an author of *Guide to the Catskills* and has updated several of Bill Hoeferlin's Hikers Regional Maps.

Among the many park and preserve officials who gave of their time

to point out the special features and activities of their areas are Kim
Estes of the Alley Pond Environmental Center; Thomas Braden and
William Vibbert of Cheesequake State Park; Gil Bergen of Con-
netquot River State Park; R. Eugene Curry and James Gibb of the
Mianus Gorge Preserve; Barry Samuels of Westchester County;
Keith R. Gunsten of New Jersey's Department of Environmental
Protection; John H. Kennedy of the New York State Office of Parks
and Recreation, Taconic Region; Nicholas Shoumatoff of Ward
Pound Ridge Reservation; Anne Marie Tytlar of the Yonkers De-
partment of Parks, Recreation, and Conservation; and Thomas Kelly
of Blue Mountain Reservation.

Many other members and friends of the Conference helped—
checking walks, locating and taking photographs, lending cars, typ-
ing, finding maps, and assisting in a myriad of other jobs. Among
these were:

Oton Ambroz	Walter Kaufman
Lenore Ballen	Kevin Kearney
Art Beach	Jonathan Kriegel
Grace Beza	Elizabeth Levers
Robert Bloom	Alexander Levine
Mrs. Rose Buchsbaum	Ted Liguori
Bob Cammann	Dick Livingston
Mary Cerulli	Jim Lober
Daniel Chazin	Dick Luttringer
Andy Coccari	Dave Lutz
Adam and Carol Cresko	Karen Mamalis
Kim Darrow	Peter Manfredonia
Don Derr	Bob Mecionis
JoAnn Dolan	Lore Oppenheimer
Ken Ettlinger	Andrew Popowich
Cynthia Fleming	Lois Raebeck
Sonia and Emanuel Fogel	Allen Walker Reid
Ellen Hitchell	Kate Rennick
Carolyn Hommel	Rita Ropes
Ben and Tina Houck	Jerry Silverstein
Debbie Jacobs	Al Smallens
Susan Jeschke	Andrew J. Smith
Jackson Jupp	Tom Stock